D0922320

MARK TWAIN

IN

WASHINGTON, D.C.

MARK TWAIN

IN

WASHINGTON, D.C.

THE ADVENTURES OF A CAPITAL CORRESPONDENT

JOHN MULLER

Forewords by Donald T. Bliss & Donald A. Ritchie

Charleston   London

THE
History
PRESS

Published by The History Press
Charleston, SC 29403
www.historypress.net

Copyright © 2013 by John Muller
All rights reserved

Front cover: Mark Twain in *Cyclopedia of American Literature*, vol. II (1875), 951. *Author's collection*. *Back cover, top left*: A photograph of Mark Twain (center), George Alfred Townsend (right) and David Gray (left) taken by Mathew Brady in his Washington, D.C. studio in February 1871. *Library of Congress*; *top right*: The Washington Monument under construction. *Library of Congress*; *bottom*: The National Hotel, at Pennsylvania Avenue and Sixth Street, NW, as carriages and people move up and down Pennsylvania Avenue in Washington, D.C. The view is toward the Capitol, with its incomplete dome, circa 1860. *Library of Congress*.

First published 2013

Manufactured in the United States

ISBN 978.1.60949.964.8

Library of Congress CIP data applied for.

Notice: The information in this book is true and complete to the best of our knowledge. It is offered without guarantee on the part of the author or The History Press. The author and The History Press disclaim all liability in connection with the use of this book.

All rights reserved. No part of this book may be reproduced or transmitted in any form whatsoever without prior written permission from the publisher except in the case of brief quotations embodied in critical articles and reviews.

To Leeroy Beebops—my brother, a captain in the United States Marine Corps and a man of several talents who, while grappling and running his way into local lore, never missed a deadline as a staff reporter for The Warrior *and set down a combination of honesty and humor in "Muller's Madness" that lives on.*

From left to right: B.A.M., Uncle G, Leeroy and Uncle Lil' Wayne.

To my thinking, Shakespeare had no more idea that he was writing for posterity than Mark Twain has at the present time, and it sometimes amuses me to think how future Mark Twain scholars will puzzle over that gentleman's present hieroglyphics and occasionally eccentric expressions.
—Charles Henry Webb, November 1865

Fame is a vapor; popularity an accident; the only earthly certainty is oblivion.
—Mark Twain upon arriving in Washington, D.C., in the winter of 1867–68

Washington news-gatherers may claim precedence in the ranks of that great American guild known as "The Press," for it is well established that metropolitan correspondents pursued their calling centuries before the discovery of the art of printing.
—Ben Perley Poore, January 1874

Contents

Foreword

Mark Twain visited Washington, D.C., many times but never stayed long. As John Muller writes, he complained about "the fickleness" of Washington's weather; it was "tricky, changeable, unreliable"—like its politics. As a teenage tourist, he wrote letters home for publication in his brother's local newspaper insightfully bemoaning how Congress failed to live up to the founders' aspirations. As a thirty-three-year-old clerk to Nevada senator William Stewart, he was a quick study, mastering the intricacies of parliamentary maneuvers and how they were used for the legislators' self-enrichment. Dismissed from his legislative post after a few weeks, he remained in town as a capital reporter and satirist, mocking legislative and bureaucratic self-importance, incompetence and corruption. In March 1868, he left Washington to launch his career as an author, taking with him a "gold mine" of anecdotes from the nation's capital that would inspire his first novel (written with *Hartford Courant* editor Charles Dudley Warner). *The Gilded Age: A Tale of Today* is a thinly veiled documentary of the scandals of the Grant Administration, illustrating the corrupting influence of money in the legislative process. It reverberates with remarkable insight and relevance to the Washington of today.

As Twain became a celebrated author, public commentator and advocate for social justice and political reform, he returned to Washington often to hobnob with the powerful, lecture, testify before Congress, advise presidents and lobby. His fiction and public commentary were greatly influenced by his Washington experiences. His friendships with presidents and influential legislators seemed undiminished by his vitriolic assault on their policies, vacuous rhetoric and self-promotion. As good politicians, perhaps they feared the power of his pen and the enormous influence on public opinion of America's first global celebrity.

Among the most quoted of public figures, Twain's aphorisms are cited for almost any proposition—often inconsistent and contradictory positions. With a handy maxim for most any occasion, he is fondly quoted by conservatives and liberals, Tea Party and Occupy Wall Street activists, libertarians and union leaders. He is an equal-opportunity satirist whose wise commentary rings true today as he exposes human frailty in the abuse of power. A passionate believer in the potential of American democracy, he is deeply concerned about how Washington politics work in practice. As Twain said, "It cannot be well or safe to let present political conditions continue indefinitely. They can be improved, and American citizenship should rise up from its disheartenment and see that this is done." Could anyone say it any better today?

Twain's few months' stay in Washington in 1867–68 was a turning point in his life. During a holiday trip to New York, he met his life partner, Livy Langdon, who would tame his frontier spirit and help discipline his inherent genius. He also received a letter from my great-grandfather, Elisha Bliss Jr., inviting him to write a book about his Quaker City tour of Europe and the Holy Lands, which launched Twain's career as a popular author who became, as *Atlantic Monthly* editor William Dean Howells labeled him, the "Lincoln of our Literature." Twain conceded that his bohemian life in Washington gave him his last days of unfettered freedom before he decided to pursue his craft with discipline and assimilate into progressive eastern society. Yet the lessons of his Washington experience greatly influenced his passion for justice and reform, expressed in his great novels, frequent lectures and political commentary.

Through his methodical research, John Muller has brought that critical time in Twain's life alive, bringing the reader into the raucous environment in which the eccentric genius became an astute student of American democracy and its flaws and potential. We learn about life in the still "raw and rugged" capital city and the disparate characters who befriended the young writer. Unearthing neglected newspaper accounts and fresh insights from local archives, Muller fills an important gap in the abundant Twain scholarship by enhancing our understanding of influences that shaped this extraordinary American icon at the critical turning point in his career.

AMBASSADOR DONALD T. BLISS (RETIRED)
Washington, D.C.

Ambassador Donald Tiffany Bliss (Retired) spent thirteen years in the federal government and thirty years practicing law in Washington, D.C. The great-grandson and grandson of Mark Twain's publishers, he wrote Mark Twain's Tale of Today, *"an expertly guided tour for the reader who seeks a unified theory of Mark Twain's politics," according to reviewer/scholar Kevin Mac Donnell. Bliss also wrote a play about Mark Twain's last years,* The Return of Halley's Comet, *and co-authored* Counsel for the Situation *with the Honorable William T. Coleman Jr.*

Foreword

Mark Twain blew in to Washington in November 1867 with a license to abuse and ridicule anyone and everybody he pleased—as well he did. He fit into the spirit of the era's Bohemian Brigade, the hard-drinking, irreverent and sardonic correspondents who had settled in the nation's capital during the Civil War and stayed through the raucous years of Reconstruction. He wrote amusing pieces for a variety of papers, experimented with giving public lectures, triumphed as an after-dinner speaker, became private secretary to a senator and developed a well-deserved reputation for cantankerousness. He also caught the eye of the Washington ladies, who admired his snowy white vests, lavender gloves and amber-hued hair. He moved repeatedly from one boardinghouse to the next, protesting the shabby furniture and shabby food. "That is Washington," he complained to his family. "I mean to keep moving." After just a few months, he breezed out of town in March 1868 as abruptly as he had arrived. That he left in the middle of the president's impeachment, the story of the year, proved that politics and journalism were only sideshows in his literary mind.

Twain's few months in Washington have been largely overlooked or underreported in the voluminous literature on his life, but it was a pivotal period in his life that deserves greater attention. Thankfully, John Muller brings this moment back front and center, using Twain's own words through the dispatches he filed and the reminiscences of his bemused peers. Twain called Washington a "bad place for a newspaperman to write a book," but he spent much of his time at the capital collecting observations on the members of Congress, reporters in the press galleries and claims agents in the lobbies who later would all play roles in his novel *The Gilded Age.*

"This is the place," he concluded, "to get a poor opinion of everybody in."

DONALD A. RITCHIE

Author of Press Gallery: Congress and the Washington Correspondents

Acknowledgements

First and foremost, thanks to God. Secondly, thanks to my mother for all her love and unpaid editing (again), B.A.M. and Leeroy. Much love to Grandma Hemmer, my New York sales agent, for the support and perfect attendance. Special thanks to Uncle G and Aunt Kathy. International love to the Alexandre Husson family. This second book would not have been possible without the ten-plus years of support of the Adult Literacy Resource Center—Marcia, Toni, Ben, Elaine, Stephon and Ms. Maxine. Meritorious thanks and recognition to the DC Public Library and my colleagues at the Washingtoniana Division.

Research is not a solitary endeavor. To uncover Mark Twain's time in Washington, I sought the assistance of many people within the network and field of Twain Studies who were kind enough to share their time. Thank you to Vic Fischer and the entire staff at the Mark Twain Project for answering my numerous calls and letter requests. Vic went out of his way to fact-check early drafts and send along unpublished material. His professionalism and responsiveness will always be appreciated and remembered. A special acknowledgement, albeit posthumously, to the foresight of the late David C. Mearns to preserve the written record of the short burst of Mark Twain's days as a capital correspondent. Thanks again to the world-class staff at various divisions of the Library of Congress, with special shouts to Patrick Kerwin of the Manuscripts Division and Amber Paranick and Gary Johnson at the Newspaper and Current Periodicals Reading Room. Thank you to John Y. Cole at the Center for the Book for his kind assistance on the history of copyright and the Library of Congress.

Acknowledgements

Barbara Schmidt of Twainquotes.com was a first responder of the first order when I stumbled upon something I didn't particularly know what to do with. Thank you for all the original work you have done in the field, the public resource you maintain and your kind help as a one-stop reference source. Thank you to Kevin Mac Donnell for your assistance and continued scholarship.

Don Bliss, a Twain scholar, was an early supporter and hung tough from start to finish when he could have easily done otherwise. Another Don, the godfather of the history of Washington City journalism, Don Ritchie, was generous enough to provide a behind-the-scenes tour of the Senate Press gallery, enabling this local neighborhood reporter to walk over the same floor that Twain did as a capital correspondent nearly 150 years ago. Thank you to both Dons for your gracious support and forewords. You are true gentlemen and scholars.

Without the help of the abovementioned and many others who shared their years of expertise and led me in the right direction to piece together the puzzle parts of Mark Twain's Washington adventures when I was going the opposite way, this book would have fallen flat. A sincere thank-you to all of you.

Additional thanks to my fellow The History Press authors and friends John DeFerrari (deserving of special recognition for being his own institution of Washington history), Garrett Peck and Dr. Ida Jones; the Glenwood Branch of the Howard County Library; the Sojourner Truth Room in the Oxon Hill Branch of the Prince George's County Library; Carol Freeman and Erin Marovelli of the Georgetown Aged Woman's Home; Jerry McCoy and the Peabody Room at the Georgetown Branch of the DC Public Library; Jim Toole of Capitol Hill Books; Bookhouse; Karen and John Thompson of Bartleby's Books; Politics & Prose; C-SPAN's Cleve Corner; Jud Ashman at the Gaithersburg Book Festival; Karen Lyon of the *Hill Rag* and Literary Hill Book Fest; Professor Saundra Maley; "Professor" Thomas Neville; Mr. Robert J. Washek; Gordon Yu for his years of steadfast counsel; Eleanor Dore for her support those many years ago and passing along a book I've since misplaced that was the genesis of this book; Stephen Powers; Georgia Avenue (my Mississippi River); Bell Clement; Blair Ruble; Brian Kraft for sharing his databases and listening to my rants; Sam Smith of the *DC Gazette*; WAMU's Rebecca Shier and Martin Austermuhle; Mike DeBonis and Chris Jenkins at the *Washington Post*; Don Rodricks at WYPR in "Bawlmore"; Danella Sealock and Teneille Gilbert at NBC-4 Washington; Nancy Olds of the *Civil War News*; my "main main," Ralph Kettell, and the entire Society of Distinguished Gentlemen—Tim Ebner, Phil Calabro and Jimmy McAndrews; Tom Cochran at Ghosts of DC; David Alpert and Dan Reed and the staff at Greater Greater Washington; my big brother, Andrew Lightman at Capital Community News; my big sister steady mobbin' 24/7/365, Caitlin Halferty; Dianne Weibe for safeguarding the legacy of George Alfred Townsend at Gathland State Park; Dan Spedden of the Maryland Department of Natural Resources; all the bookstores; everyone at The History Press (extra appreciation to Katie Parry, Sarah Falter, Hilary Parrish, Jaime Muehl, Dani McGrath, Meredith Riddick, Will Collicott and the ever-patient and faithful Hannah Cassilly); all reporters who hit the city streets with steadfast fury and researchers kicking up dust; and my godmother, Adrienne Washington, for the ragged start in this journalism game. If I missed anyone, I'm not hard to find.

Preface

Seven or eight years ago, I was reviewing a vertical file at the Historical Society of Washington in the Old Carnegie Library and came across a clipping that included Mark Twain's quotes on the city from his 1854 visit (when he was still Samuel Clemens). Before then, I had never heard that Mark Twain had visited Washington, D.C. The limited knowledge I had of Mark Twain was as the author of *Adventures of Huckleberry Finn*, *The Prince and the Pauper*, *A Connecticut Yankee in King Arthur's Court* and the omnipresent man in the white suit whose style Tom Wolfe emulated. A few years out of high school, my worldview was narrow—Twain was similar to Clint Eastwood in that he had always been presented to me as an old and cantankerous spirit, never having lived or enjoyed any sort of youth.

Shortly thereafter, I was browsing a discarded antiquarian book at the Martin Luther King Jr. Memorial Library about the history of American literature. (Being young and hence careless, I sadly misplaced the book.) The volume featured profiles of Walt Whitman, John Greenleaf Whittier, Mark Twain and others. According to the book, some of the most prominent American men of letters, including Mark Twain, had a common thread: they had come up through the ranks as journalists. I did not know it at the time, but I can look back now and realize that moment as the origin of this book.

For the past four years, I have been a journalist in Washington writing for print and online publications. I am a local reporter. A couple of years back, I presented a panel at the annual Washington, D.C. Historical Studies Conference on the history of newspapers and journalism in Washington.

During this process, I came back to the vertical file that included the mention of Twain's 1854 visit and learned through further research that he had been a journalist in Washington in the winter of 1867–68.

In the fall of 2012, my first book, *Frederick Douglass in Washington, D.C.: The Lion of Anacostia*, was published by The History Press. Within a matter of weeks, I was on contract to write a second book to explore Mark Twain's days as a capital correspondent. I was unaware of what I was getting into. Although I made an initial survey in the early fall of 2012 into databases, bibliographies and other sources to confirm that no book had singularly explored Twain's time in Washington, I missed Don Bliss's book, *Mark Twain's Tale of Today: Halley's Comet Returns—The Celebrated Author Critiques American Politics*, which was published by CreateSpace in late September 2012. Don and I subsequently got in touch, and Don expressed his support, which I will always be thankful for.

As I began to research Twain, I felt the cliché from *Jaws* applied to my initial efforts: "You're going to need a bigger boat." At this time, interest in the Douglass book began to take off, to my pleasant surprise, but consumed me for whole days at a time. Fortunately, unlike that of Douglass, I found the field of Twain studies includes a quadrennial conference, multiple annual scholarly publications, an international listserv, member-based organizations with local chapters throughout the country, independent public scholars such as Barbara Schmidt, an online book-review forum and an incredibly responsive and rather unified group of collaborative scholars from academics to rare book dealers. It was a lifeboat.

There have been hundreds of books on Mark Twain, from full-length biographies to more intimate studies that focus on his time in Hannibal (Missouri), Virginia City (Nevada), San Francisco, Hartford (Connecticut), Buffalo, Elmira (New York), Vienna (Austria) and elsewhere. There have been anthologies of his books, short stories, personal letters and interviews; studies of his relationships with his publisher, presidents, brother, other writers and God; psychological profiles; works of literary criticism; and more. As a rather novice historian, I know of no undertaking as vast as that of the Mark Twain Project. The Mark Twain Project Online, according to its website, "applies innovative technology to more than four decades' worth of archival research by expert editors at the Mark Twain Project. It offers unfettered, intuitive access to reliable texts, accurate and exhaustive notes, and the most recently discovered letters and documents. Its ultimate purpose is to produce a digital critical edition, fully annotated, of everything Mark Twain wrote." It was a lifesaver.

As Adam Gopnik wrote in late 2010 in the *New Yorker*, "There was a time, now long forgotten, when Mark Twain was frankly regarded as a failure." When Twain arrived in Washington City in 1867, he was on the cusp of success, although it was in no way assured, as Twain painfully realized. Despite his growing journalistic recognition, he still anxiously chased financial success. While in Washington, his literary reach expanded through the newspaper exchange system. This was also when he was first approached about writing a full-length book, which appealed to his ambition and his wallet. Twain's stay in Washington was short—less than four months—but arguably one of the more pivotal points in his career.

With the publication in the fall of 2010 of the surprise best-selling *Autobiography of Mark Twain: The Complete and Authoritative Edition Volume 1* and the publication of *Volume 2* this fall, the Mark Twain industry will surely keep growing. Add this book to the production line, assembled in less than a year.

While I was unable to make a trip to Berkeley to visit the Mark Twain Papers, with the remote assistance of Victor Fischer and others, previously unpublished material is presented in this paperback. Working through sources at the Library of Congress, the Special Collections of the DC Public Library and the archives of Gathland State Park in Maryland, I have endeavored to introduce fresh information of interest to Washingtonians and Twainians alike. I take full responsibility for all errors and oversights in existing scholarship. Due to word count and publication restraints, my more than five hundred endnotes of more than ten thousand words are not included in this edition. The good folks within the field of Twain studies take scholarship seriously; so do I. Two copies of the endnoted text are publicly available for reference at the Washingtoniana Room of the Martin Luther King Jr. Memorial Library and at the Kiplinger Research Library at the Historical Society of Washington in the Old Carnegie Library. For those wishing to contact me directly, please feel free to email me at MarkTwainInDC@gmail.com. I will respond within ten business days.

My use of "Twain," with the exception of content that pre-dates February 1863, in reference to Samuel Clemens is deliberate and should not be interpreted as an argument for or against his duality or singularity of character. While in Washington, Twain was a character—that is the only story I attempt to tell.

JOHN MULLER
August 2013

CHAPTER 1

Such Is Life, and Such Is Washington!

Then, if you should be seized with a desire to go to the Capitol, or somewhere else, you may stand in a puddle of water, with the snow driving in your face for fifteen minutes or more, before an omnibus rolls lazily by; and when one does come, ten to one there are nineteen passengers inside and fourteen outside, and while the driver casts on you a look of commiseration, you have the inexpressible satisfaction of knowing that you closely resemble a very moist dishrag (and feel so, too) at the same time that you are unable to discover what benefit you have derived from your fifteen minutes' soaking; and so, driving your fists into the inmost recesses of your breeches pockets, you stride away in despair, with a step and a grimace that would make the fortune of a tragedy actor, while your "onery" appearance is greeted with "screams of laftur" from a pack of vagabond boys over the way. Such is life, and such is Washington!
—Samuel L. Clemens, February 1854

I n 1909, the penultimate year of Mark Twain's life, he stood on the platform of the B&O Railroad station in Baltimore, Maryland. Long familiar with the rhythms of travel, he had logged thousands of miles over the years traveling across the United States, Europe, Australia, Japan, the Middle East and Africa. While waiting for his return train to New York, the world-weary traveler's mind wandered. Here, fifty-five years before, as a wet-behind-the ears small-town chap, he had had to make a run for it, he told his friend and biographer Albert Bigelow Paine. The teenaged Twain had just barely managed to change cars en route to his maiden voyage to the raw and rugged Washington City, a relative backwoods.

When the young Twain first arrived in the city in February 1854, both were rough around the edges and of dubious potential. Founded by an act of Congress in 1792, the nation's capital city was a curiosity among European and American travelers and writers. Previously meeting in Annapolis, Philadelphia, Trenton and New York City like itinerant preachers, Congress permanently convened the seat of the United States government in Washington in November 1800.

The location of today's city avenues, circles, streets and boundary stones reflect what was laid out by a team of surveyors and planners, including Benjamin Banneker, Pierre Charles L'Enfant and Andrew Ellicott. Out of the wilderness, plantation fields and the port city of Georgetown, the nation's federal square was constituted.

"We only need here houses, cellars, kitchens, scholarly men, amiable women, and a few other such trifles, to possess a perfect city. In a word, this is the best city in the world to live in—in the future," Gouverneur Morris, New York Senator and member of the first Congress to hold session in Washington, wrote of the nation's capital city two centuries ago.

One of the first books to describe the municipal outpost, *A Chronological and Statistical Description of the District of Columbia*, written and published in Paris by David B. Warden in 1816, prefaces its intro: "A publication of this kind is now called for, not only by citizens of the United States but also by foreigners, who, from motives of curiosity or interest, seek minute information concerning the present state of the American metropolis."

Warden cited local lore that held that the city was destined to become as respectable as the great capitals of Europe: "The origin of Washington, like that of several ancient cities, is already wrapt [*sic*] in fable." Legend held "that a few families had lived there in rural solitude for nearly a century, of which one was established on the borders of the Columbia Creek, from whom it received the name of Tiber; and the place of residence was called Rome." Fact or fiction, it was believed into the twentieth century "that a man by the name of Pope settled on Capitol Hill in the middle of the Seventeenth Century" and had called the area Rome. "History may hereafter record the belief that this simple farmer, endowed with prophetical powers, foresaw the destinies of the Columbian territory."

Visions of the future abounded in this planned political center; a country's capital city rising out of nothing was an uncommon event, especially in the New World. Visitors who embarked to the city with any expectations whatsoever were not impressed.

"Travellers [*sic*], from different motives, have given very unfaithful pictures of the city of Washington," Warden contested. "The buildings are described to be in a state of dilapidation. The inhabitants are represented as a 'half-organised, half-minded race;' although it is well known, that they came from various regions of the United States and from different countries of Europe, bringing with them qualities of mind and body, and topographical habits, which prevent the possibility of any characteristic trait, except in the imagination of the poet."

Passing through Washington during Jefferson's first administration, Irish poet Tom Moore committed his thoughts to satirical verse:

> *This fam'd metropolis, where fancy sees*
> *Squares in morasses, obelisks in trees;*
> *Which travelling fools, and gazetteers adorn*
> *With shrines unbuilt, and heroes yet unborn;*
> *Tho' nought but wood and—they see,*
> *Where streets should run, and sages ought to be.*

Writing his father in January 1832, Alexis de Tocqueville summarized the city's failure to live up to its grand ambitions:

A visit to Washington gives one some idea of how wonderfully well-equipped men are to calculate future events. Forty years ago, when choosing a capital for the Union became a matter of public concern, the first step, reasonably enough, was to decide upon the most favorable location. The place chosen was a vast plain along the banks of the Potomac. This wide, deep river bordering one end would bring European goods to the new city; fertile fields on the other side would keep markets well provisioned and nourish a large population. People

Alexis de Tocqueville passed through Washington in January 1832 on his tour of America en route to writing *Democracy in America*. *Library of Congress.*

assumed that in twenty years Washington would be the hub of the Union's internal and external commerce. It was bound, in due course, to have a million inhabitants. Anticipating this influx, the government began to raise public edifices and lay out enormously wide streets. Trees that might have hindered the construction of houses were felled by the acre.

All was for naught. De Tocqueville determined, "The population didn't come; vessels did not sail up the Potomac. Today, Washington presents the image of an arid plain scorched by the sun, on which, scattered here and there, are two or three sumptuous edifices and five or six villages that constitute the city. Unless one is Alexander or Peter the Great, one should not get involved in creating the capital of an empire." Upon returning to France, de Tocqueville published his famous work *Democracy in America*. His summary of Washington presented a city still taking form.

Outside the rugged new capital of Washington, American institutions and culture in the rest of the country had been progressing since colonial times and were more fully formed. One of de Tocqueville's larger observations of the country was that of the culture and profession of journalism. He wrote, "In America, there is scarcely a hamlet which has not its own newspaper. It may readily be imagined that neither discipline nor unity of design can be communicated to so multifarious a host, and each one is consequently led to fight under his own standard. All the political journals of the United States are arrayed indeed on the side of the administration or against it; but they attack and defend in a thousand different ways."

In Europe, journalists mainly came from the aristocratic families, while in America, freedom of the press was a democratic right that was fully exercised by men from all walks of life. De Tocqueville decided, "The facility with which journals can be established induces a multitude of individuals to take part in them; but as the extent of competition precludes the possibility of considerable profit, the most distinguished classes of society are rarely led to engage in these undertakings. But such is the number of the public prints that, even if they were a source of wealth, writers of ability could not be found to direct them all. The journalists of the United States are usually placed in a very humble position with a scanty education and a vulgar turn of mind."

When the parliamentarian reporter-turned-novelist Charles Dickens visited Washington City, he was restrained in his critique of the burgeoning metropolis. "Burn the whole down; build it up again in wood and plaster; widen it a little," Dickens wrote in his 1842 *American Notes for General Circulation*. The American capital was austere, unlike the old world European capital cities. "[P]lough up all the roads; plant a great deal of coarse turf in every place where it ought not to be; erect three handsome buildings in stone and marble, anywhere, but the more entirely out of everybody's way the better; call one the Post Office; one the Patent Office, and one the Treasury; make it scorching hot in the morning, and freezing cold in the afternoon, with an occasional tornado of wind and dust; leave a brick-field without the bricks, in all central places where a street may naturally be expected: and that's Washington."

To Dickens, the city was incomplete: "Spacious avenues, that begin in nothing and lead nowhere; streets, mile-long, that only want houses, roads and inhabitants; public buildings that need but a public to be complete; and ornaments of great thoroughfares, which only lack great thoroughfares to ornament—are its leading features." For successive generations, a phrase of Dickens's critique of Washington has lived on in the classrooms of city students: "It is sometimes called the City of Magnificent Distances, but it might with greater propriety be termed the City of Magnificent Intentions."

In February 1854, the feet of a headstrong Missouri teenager first hit the muddy ground and his eyes took in their inaugural gaze of the capital city. Through the static of snow, he saw nearly the same unrealized metropolis Alexander de Tocqueville and Charles Dickens had visited and chronicled in the previous decades. While Dickens and de Tocqueville were of old European extraction and looked at the city with a natural detachment, this runaway itinerant printer from the hinterlands of the new country saw the city with the hope and optimism characteristic of the New World; he saw it not for what it was but what it could be. "Like America, Washington must be judged only by looking to its future—that great future which we of this generation are destined to see only with prophetic eyes," intoned *Harper's Monthly Magazine* in December 1852.

The young Samuel Clemens could hardly have foreseen what would become of his life or the direction the capital city would take, but the teenager's infatuation would commence a love/hate relationship that would span more than half a century. Washington City was a curiosity to both native and foreigner visitors. Leaving his home in Hannibal, Missouri, in May 1853, Clemens traveled to St. Louis, New York and Philadelphia before passing through Washington in February 1854. Clemens wanted to see the city for himself and, like any skeptical American teenager, form his own independent opinion.

Alighting from a railcar at the Italianate-styled Baltimore and Ohio Railroad Passenger Depot, which had just opened months before at the

Samuel Clemens, circa 1851. *Mark Twain Papers, UC Berkeley.*

corner of New Jersey Avenue and C Street NW, Clemens hastened to take a room in one of the avenue's hotels. On the morning of February 17, the eighteen-year-old hit the city streets for the first time, walking through a snowstorm. "I started toward the capitol, but there being no sidewalk, I sank ankle deep in mud and snow at every step. When at last I reached the capitol, I found that Congress did not sit till 11 o'clock; so I thought I would stroll around the city for an hour or two," he reported to his brother Orion's newspaper, the *Muscatine Journal.*

He reversed his course, retracing his steps up Pennsylvania Avenue, where he admired the "pretty edifice" of the Treasury Building, "with a long row of columns in front" and adjacent to the White House. Clemens passed into Lafayette Square, where he made note of an artistic and technological feat unseen before in the country: "I amused myself with a gaze at Clark Mills' great equestrian statue of Jackson. It is a beautiful thing, and well worth a long walk on a stormy day to see." Erected to public fanfare in January 1853, the statue had been cast from bronze cannons captured by Andrew Jackson during the War of 1812 and depicted the general doffing his cap on a rearing horse. It was the first of its kind, an engineering achievement not yet accomplished before in American sculpture. Mills would later cast the Statue of Freedom, which was installed atop the crown of the Capitol in 1863, where it has rested since. The Jackson statue remains in Lafayette Square today, framing an iconic image of the White House looking down Sixteenth Street NW.

Clemens's observations of the physical city mirrored those of Dickens. Two- and three-story brick houses on Pennsylvania Avenue appeared as though they had "been scattered abroad by the winds. There are scarcely any pavements, and I might almost say no gas, off the thoroughfare." Tired and now soaked from the snow, Clemens sought to catch one of the city's omnibuses back down Pennsylvania Avenue to the Capitol.

In February 1854, eighteen-year-old Samuel Clemens noted C. Wright Mills's statue of Andrew Jackson in Lafayette Square, across the street from the White House. Dedicated in 1853, it was the first equestrian statue ever installed in the United States. *Library of Congress*.

During Clemens's visit, a system of three omnibus lines ran in Washington, connecting the Navy Yard to Georgetown. This network paled in comparison to New York's system. In January, the *Daily Evening Star* reported that New York ran "33 lines of omnibuses, with 521 stages, and five railroads, with 164 cars—of which the New Haven and Harlem road has 13; Sixth Avenue road, 43; Eighth Avenue road, 50; Second Avenue road, 50; Second Avenue road, 18; and Third Avenue road, 40 cars." Clemens waited for "fifteen minutes or more" before an omnibus headed for the Capitol with "nineteen passengers inside and fourteen outside" rolled by "lazily." The driver gave Clemens a "look

A view of lower Pennsylvania Avenue and the U.S. Capitol in the early 1850s from *Appleton's Northern & Eastern Traveler's Guide. Author's collection.*

of commiseration" and continued without stopping. Disheartened, the young man put his "fists into the inmost recesses" of his "breeches pockets" and strode back down Pennsylvania Avenue with "a step and grimace that would make the fortune of a tragedy actor." Across the way, "a pack of vagabond boys" mocked Clemens. Relatively forgotten in a modern telling of the city's history, Clemens's experiences and frustrations with the omnibus are not dissimilar from riders of today's Metro. The omnibus begat the streetcar, first running in Washington during the Civil War in 1862, which ran for a century until 1962, which would beget the Metro, which opened to the public on March 27, 1976.

Reaching the Capitol, Clemens passed through the hall between the Senate and House chambers, "embellished with numerous large paintings, portraying some of the principal events in American history," before taking his seat in the Senate Chamber to "see the men who give the people the benefit of their wisdom and learning for a little glory." However, the deliberative body's past "glory hath departed." Gone were Henry Clay, Daniel Webster and John C. Calhoun.

The senators were not ostentatious in their dress or manners and only spoke when they had "something to say." Lewis Cass was a "fine-looking

HALL OF THE HOUSE OF REPRESENTATIVES.

THE SENATE CHAMBER, WASHINGTON.

Hall of the House of Representatives and the Senate Chamber, circa 1854. *Author's collection.*

old man; Mr. [Stephen] Douglass [*sic*], or 'Young America,' looks like a lawyer's clerk, and Mr. Seward is a slim, dark, bony individual and looks like a respectable wind would blow him out of the country." During Clemens's visit to the Senate, Seward, who would later lose the 1860 Republican presidential primary to Abraham Lincoln and serve as both Lincoln's and Andrew Johnson's secretary of state, spoke for three hours in support of the Missouri Compromise.

The decorum of the Senate disappeared when Clemens visited the people's body. "In the House, nearly every man seemed to have something weighing on his mind on which the salvation of the Republic depended, and which he appeared very anxious to ease himself of; and so there were generally half a dozen of them on the floor, and 'Mr. Chairman! Mr. Chairman!' was echoed from every part of the house," Clemens reported. Thomas Hart Benton, who had served for nearly thirty years in the Senate representing Missouri and now represented Missouri's first Congressional district, was detached and disinterested, providing the young journalist no colorful copy: "Mr. Benton sits silent and gloomy in the midst of the din, like a lion imprisoned in a cage of monkeys, who, feeling his superiority, disdains to notice their chattering." After observing all there was to see at the Capitol and now dried out, Clemens headed back to his room and readied for another day exploring the city.

On the following day, February 19, Clemens began his correspondence describing the Smithsonian Institution's "large, fine building" that "looks like a half-church and half-castle." Along with its gallery of paintings and thirty-two-thousand-volume library, the yet-to-be-completed castle contained a popular lecture hall that could seat two thousand people.

Piquing the teenaged Clemens's intellectual interest was the Museum of the Patent Office, holding "by far the largest collection of curiosities in the United States." Foreshadowing his lifelong fascination with the emerging technologies of his time—from the telephone to the typewriter to the dictograph—and his failed pursuits at invention that nearly ruined him and his family financially, Clemens "spent a very pleasant four hours…looking at the thousands upon thousands of wonders it contains." He looked at "Peruvian mummies of great antiquity, autographs of Bonaparte and several kings of Europe, pagan idols, and part of the costumes of Atahualpa and Cortes" among homegrown war relics such as a "suit of clothes worn by Washington when he resigned his commission as Commander-in-Chief of the American forces; the coat worn by Jackson at the Battle of New Orleans; Washington's sword, war-tent" and other "camp equipage." However, his

Clemens spent hours exploring "by far the largest collection of curiosities in the United States," held in the Patent Office, today the National Portrait Gallery. *Author's collection.*

real interest was a "printing press used by Franklin, in London, nearly one hundred and twenty years ago."

Becoming a printer's apprentice in the late 1840s for his hometown paper, Clemens had an intricate knowledge of the machine. After describing its outdated process, he wrote, "This press is capable of printing about 125 sheets per hour; and after seeing it, I have watched Hoe's great machine, throwing off its 20,000 sheets in the same space of time, with an interest I never felt before."

On his trip East, Clemens had worked for a time as a journeyman printer in Philadelphia. Although Clemens thought his hands were fast at typesetting, he saw his country weeklies hadn't prepared him for the demand of the big-city dailies. It was in Philadelphia that Richard Hoe's "rotary-style press" had been "first put into use, in 1846, by the Philadelphia Public Ledger." In subsequent years, the machine became "widely adopted by the other metropolitan papers." At the time of Clemens's sojourn, the *National Intelligencer* (a paper Clemens would later critique) was the leading daily, as the *Evening Star* had been printed for just over a year. As the editors of

Volume 1 of Mark Twain's letters note, "The fact that Clemens observed a Hoe press at work in a Washington newspaper office may suggest that he had been looking for work." If Clemens had sought work, it's likely he stopped in at the offices of the *National Intelligencer* at the northwest corner of Seventh and D Streets, where the paper was published by Joseph Gales and William W. Seaton from 1818 to 1865.

Writing in the *Records of the Columbia Historical Society*, Allen C. Clark notes, "For thirty years, Mr. Gales from his country seat, Eckington, came to the offices on a closed carriage. Between carriage door and office door he was frequently importuned by a mendicant, whom he never denied. He had a noble dog of great size who carried the mail in a basket to the post office. His master was a Whig, and he was a Whig dog. He welcomed a Whig and frowned upon a Democrat. When the election of General Taylor was announced his tail had a joyous wag, and when the election of Mr. Buchannan [*sic*] was announced the tail had no wag at all."

Construction began on the Washington Monument in 1848 and was not completed until 1885. Clemens visited the half-built obelisk in 1854, which remained an "ungainly old chimney" when he returned to the city as a capital correspondent in the winter of 1867–68. *Library of Congress.*

Leaving the Patent Office, which today blankets an entire city block between F and G Streets and Seventh and Ninth Streets and houses the National Portrait Gallery and the Smithsonian American Art Museum, Clemens eyed the uncompleted Washington Monument. In that day's edition of the *National Intelligencer*, there was a call for donations to complete the monument.

Before signing off on his first Washington correspondence, Clemens observed that Washington had one theater of consequence: the National Theatre. On the evening of February 17, Clemens was part of a "good audience" that saw the famed tragedian Edwin Forrest portray Othello for the "first and only time." It was unnecessary to mention that Forrest was white and had performed the role in black face; it was implied.

In *The Ordeal of Mark Twain*, published in 1920, literary critic Van Wyck Brooks argues that as a young man, Clemens displayed "never a hint of melancholy, of aspiration, of hope, depression, joy, even ambition. His letters are full of statistics as the travel reports of an engineer and the only sensation he seems to experience is the tell-tale sensation of home-sickness. He has no wish to investigate life."

Twain was a provincial teenager when he first came to Washington and inspected the city as his own tour guide. Even if they had formed any clear opinions at that age, most teenagers would not have had enough confidence to espouse them. Reporting the facts is safe, and perhaps Orion wanted the facts only, not some teenager's half-formed opinions. By the time Twain returned to Washington, he was nearly twice as old and had traveled thousands of miles from the western edge of the New World to the Biblical ruins of the Old World. His writing apprenticeship had progressed from simply remarking on the rich material of frontier life in the Nevada silver-mining towns and cosmopolitan life in San Francisco, where he reportedly took part in a "'hasheesh' mania," to humor and social commentary. He was progressively sharpening his pen to a razor edge, which he would wield with increasing maturity, sophistication and well-honed wit. To compare the backwoods teenaged Clemens of 1854, who had mostly just set the type for newspapers, to the mature, well-traveled Twain of 1867, who had composed hundreds of local newspaper columns, sketches and travel letters for newspapers and was now contemplating composing books, is unreasonable.

CHAPTER 2

Mark Twain Comes to Washington

Don't make any arrangements about lecturing for me. I have got a better thing in Washington. Shall spend the winter there.
—*Samuel Clemens to Frank Fuller, August 7, 1867*

When South Carolina left the Union on December 20, 1860, Samuel Clemens, then twenty-five, was copiloting a steamboat on the Mississippi River. Although his father, John Marshall Clemens, had owned slaves, Clemens, along with his Yankee-bred copilot, "was strong for the Union." However, "a month later, the secession atmosphere had considerably thickened on the Lower Mississippi," and Clemens now decided he was, in fact, "a rebel." Departing from New Orleans, which joined the Confederate cause in late January 1861, Clemens returned to his boyhood home in Hannibal, Missouri.

During the early months of 1861, "the first wash of the wave of war broke upon the shores of Missouri." Clemens's home state was invaded by Union forces, including Ulysses S. Grant, who took possession of St. Louis, thus controlling the northern Mississippi River. In response, the governor issued a proclamation that called for 50,000 militiamen to repel the Northern invaders. By the end of the war, Missouri contributed 109,000 men to the Union army and an estimated 30,000 to the Confederacy in the form of enlistments and irregularly formed outfits.

Swept up in a sense of adventure, Clemens, with a gang of fifteen of his childhood friends, gathered "in a secret place by night and formed ourselves into a militia company." Clemens was selected as a second lieutenant in the Marion Rangers, named for the county of Marion. Armed with a "shabby old shot gun" but no real desire or inclination to use it, Clemens was admittedly more a rabbit than a soldier. Unable and unwilling to lead men into war, Clemens deserted the Confederate cause. Writing twenty-four years later, he recalled, "I knew more about retreating than the man that invented retreating."

Upon arriving home, Clemens learned that his older brother, Orion, whom he had worked for as a printer and occasional correspondent, "had just been appointed Secretary of Nevada Territory—an office of such majesty that it concentrated in itself the duties and dignities of Treasurer, Comptroller, Secretary of State, and Acting Governor in the Governor's absence." Orion had been mentored by President Lincoln's new attorney general, Edward Bates, since the late 1840s and had stumped for the

Wells Fargo & Co.'s Express Office on C Street in Virginia City, Nevada, circa 1866. Nearby were the offices for the *Territorial Enterprise*, where Samuel Clemens got his start as a journalist and adopted the pen name Mark Twain. *Library of Congress*.

Lincoln ticket in northern Missouri in the election of 1860. As a reward for Orion's efforts, Bates wrote Secretary of State William Seward on March 12, barely a week after Lincoln's inauguration, conveying Orion's request to be appointed "the post of a Secretary." In Bates's tepid commendation, he said, "I consider him an honest man of fair mediocrity of talents & learning— more indeed of both than I have seen in several Territorial secretaries." Without a sense "of being very urgent," Bates concluded that Orion would "be grateful for a favor." On March 27, Orion found that the appointment of secretary of the Nevada Territory was his.

Although the position reportedly paid a salary of $1,800 a year, Orion did not have money for the overland stage. His younger brother, Samuel, did. In "cold blood," Orion offered Samuel the "sublime position of private secretary under him," which was accepted. Once in Carson City, Nevada, Samuel quickly became disinterested in his "unique sinecure" as "private secretary to his majesty the Secretary," for there "was not yet writing enough for two of us." Looking for "amusement," Clemens began a year's worth of prospecting that promised great riches one day and penury the next. He became "smitten with the silver fever" with the daily sight of ore emerging from the mills of the Comstock Lode.

In February 1862, while working as a pocket miner, Clemens "amused" himself by sending irregular "letters to the chief paper of the territory, the Virginia Daily *Territorial Enterprise*." In the fall, he received an offer of twenty-five dollars a week to become the city editor of the *Enterprise*. Although the money was "a bloated luxury," Clemens was unsure of his suitability, due to his "inexperience and consequent unfitness for the position." Self-sufficient since he was thirteen and afraid of being dead broke, Clemens "was scared into being a city editor."

Under the guidance of founding editor Joseph Goodman, Clemens quickly got his bearings. Clemens soon ingratiated himself into his new locale. "I struck up friendships with the reporters of the other journals, and we swapped 'regulars' with each other and thus economized work. 'Regulars' are permanent sources of news," he wrote nearly a decade later in *Roughing It*. At the forefront of enterprising journalism in the Old West, where red blood became black ink, Clemens was a leading figure. The activity in Virginia City, with an estimated fifteen to eighteen thousand people, was endless and copy bountiful, as there were "military companies, fire companies, brass-bands, banks, hotels, theaters, 'hurdy-gurdy houses,' wide-open gambling palaces, political pow-wows, civic processions, street-fights, murders, inquest, riots, a whisky mill every fifteen steps, a Board of

Aldermen, a Mayor, a City Surveyor, a City Engineer, a Chief of the Fire Department, with First, Second, and Third Assistant, a Chief of Police, City Marshal, and a large police force, two Boards of Mining Brokers, a dozen breweries, and a half dozen jails and station-houses in full operation, and some talk of building a church."

Covering his share of vice, the mines, ghost stories, social functions and other intrigues (sometimes imaginary) in his local columns, Clemens began reporting on the territorial legislature and courts in December 1862. In a letter from Carson City to the *Enterprise* published on February 3, 1863, detailing a lavish party that had kept him "awake for forty-eight hours," Clemens signed off, "Yours dreamily, MARK TWAIN." This is the first known appearance of the *nom de plume* that would alter the course of American literature.

Toward the closing months of 1863, Twain, who regularly had his items in the *Enterprise* re-published in papers throughout the region, began contributing to *The Golden Era*, a literary journal out of San Francisco. One of his earliest contributions was "The Great Prize Fight," which satirized a boxing match of "extraordinary importance" between California governor Leland Stanford and Governor-Elect Frederick Ferdinand Low for a purse of $100,000. The two pugilists were being trained by the associate justice of the U.S. Supreme Court, Stephen Field, previously the chief justice of California, and "Hon Wm. M. Stewart (commonly called 'Bill Stewart' or 'Bullyragging Bill Stewart') of the city of Virginia, the most popular as well as the most distinguished lawyer in Nevada Territory, member of the Constitutional Convention, and future U.S. Senator." After going toe-to-toe for five rounds, each camp "threw up their sponges simultaneously," and the match was pronounced a draw.

Establishing a growing literary reputation, in December 1863, Twain was elected "President of the Convention" of the Third House, an eccentric group of journalists, lawyers, bohemians and businessmen who mocked the legislative process. Stewart was among the attendees who reportedly engaged in a back-and-forth with Chairman Twain. At this same time, an "event of significance in the Western development of Mark Twain occur[red]," according to scholar Ivan Benson.

Charles F. Browne, who wrote articles for the *Plain Dealer* in Ohio under the pen name Artemus Ward, was in town, according to Twain, to "deliver his lectures and perhaps make some additions to the big sho'." During Ward's three-week sojourn in Virginia City, he and Twain "went roof-walking, and had a gay time jumping from one roof down to the other."

While in Nevada, Mark Twain covered the territorial legislature and constitutional convention and was president of the "Third House," a group of journalists who mocked the legislative process. *Mark Twain Papers, UC Berkeley*.

On a more serious note, Ward advised Twain "to work into the Eastern publications immediately" and wrote him a letter of introduction to the *New York Sunday Mercury*'s editor that resulted in two of Twain's pieces being published in February 1864. Despite Ward's urging to seek a larger audience, Twain remained in Nevada. In January 1864, he began covering his second legislative session in Carson City. As Benson notes, this "assignment is of great significance in Mark Twain's career, for he became during this reporting period a really important figure in public affairs. Now his writings, although mostly still in a humorous vein, carry weight with the readers. There is almost invariably to be found in them some element of political or social criticism. His satire and irony are now being directed toward problems of some real importance in the life of the community."

Previously writing about the nonexistent fossil of a petrified man and imaginary massacres in which whole families were killed, Twain now wrote on subjects of consequence and became "less ephemeral and much less coarse." His prominence as a raconteur continued to grow. After addressing an assemblage of the Third House, he was given a gold watch. With his respectability seemingly on the rise, Twain made an error that would require him to leave the "Washoe," an area in the Carson Valley of Nevada and California.

"In May 1864, a group of Virginia City's feminine elite decided to put on a masquerade ball to raise money for the U.S. Sanitary Commission," writes a Twain biographer. "After the ball, however, the ladies," which included Twain's sister-in-law, "decided to put the money to another use." Composing his copy inebriated, Twain speculated that the money would be sent "to aid a Miscegenation Society somewhere in the East." Although his editor, Goodman, warned against its publication, it made its way into print. It was swiftly denounced as a "rumor" and "hoax" in a subsequent editorial in the *Enterprise*. An additional dispute during "Twain's last editorial controversy on the Comstock Lode" was that members of the rival paper, the *Virginia Daily Union*, had not donated their fair share to the benefit. A sharp war of expositions ensued, with Twain attacking editor James L. Laird and Laird counterattacking. According to Benson, Twain was now in trouble in both Virginia City with his fellow journalists and in "Carson City with the leading women of society." After it was thought that a challenge to a duel (which was illegal) had been insinuated, Twain left for San Francisco in May 1864.

Twain transitioned into the bohemian culture of San Francisco with a job, at the rate of thirty-five dollars a week, with the *Morning Call*, which he was dissatisfied with "[f]rom the first" because of his position as "merely another staff member." Notwithstanding his frustrations, Twain was now in the close company of the literary *avant garde*. Over the next three and a half years, he would write for a series of daily papers—*Morning Call, San Francisco Dramatic Chronicle, Sacramento Daily Union, San Francisco Bulletin, San Francisco Alta California*—and the literary journals *The Golden Era* and *The Californian*.

Although living scattershot, Twain realized his calling during this period. Writing in October 1865 to his brother Orion, who would commence a life's worth of struggles after being passed over for an appointment to Nevada's state government, which was constituted in the fall of 1864, Twain instructed, "You had better shove this in the stove, for if we strike a bargain, I don't want any absurd 'literary remains' & 'unpublished letters of Mark Twain' published after I am planted." According to Twain, "I never had but two powerful ambitions in my life. One was to be a pilot, & the other a

San Francisco, circa 1865, where Mark Twain was a reporter after leaving Nevada. *Library of Congress.*

preacher of the gospel. I accomplished the one & failed in the other because I could not supply myself with the necessary stock in trade—i.e. religion. I have given it up forever. I never had a 'call' in that direction, anyhow, & my aspirations were the very ecstasy of presumption. But I have had a 'call' to literature, of a low order—i.e. humorous."

However confident a front Twain might have presented to his family, all was not well with his psyche. He closed his letter by stating, "If I do not get out of debt in 3 months—pistols or poison for one—exit me." According to a personal notation made more than forty years later, Twain recollected that in 1866, he had "put the pistol to my head but wasn't man enough to pull the trigger. Many times I have been sorry I did not succeed, but I was never ashamed of having tried."

Although bedeviled by suicidal thoughts, Twain found his luck slowly turning the corner. In the November 18, 1865 issue of *The Saturday Press*, an alternative weekly published out of New York, Twain achieved what would become his first big literary success with his story "Jim Smiley and His Jumping Frog." The story, a riff on an older tale of American folklore, was widely re-published throughout the country. By March 1866, Twain was bound for the Sandwich Islands, present-day Hawaii, on contract for the *Sacramento Union* to write "twenty or thirty letters." According to biographer Ron Powers, Twain "soaked up character, incident, anecdote, language, physical terrain, and local myth" and managed to break a nationwide story of the survivors of a shipwreck. His four-month stay would provide Twain with exotic lecture material for years to come.

Returning to the mainland, Twain's first test at turning his writing for the page into a performance for the stage was at San Francisco's Maguire's Academy of Music on October 2, 1866. The bill famously promoted the "Trouble to Begin at 8 o'clock." Twain planted "three old friends…[who] had agreed to laugh lustily at the bare suggestion of a witticism" in the audience. His career as a lecturer began with a thunderclap. To positive review, he gave seventeen subsequent lectures throughout California and Nevada before the close of the year. In December of 1866 Twain headed east, where, when not spending long stretches of time overseas, he would remain the rest of his life. After twenty-seven days at sea, Twain touched down in New York on January 12. He had big-city dreams in his head and in the palm of his hand. Like many teenagers, early experiences had left an oversized impression; Twain had not forgotten his first visit to the big city. Before traveling on to Washington City in 1854, a seventeen-year-old Clemens had spent time in antebellum New York. As Powers wrote in his 2005 biography, "[Twain] knew this town and what it could do for a fellow with moxie." In Twain's own words, written in his adulthood, "Make your mark in New York, and you are a made man."

On a mission to publish his first book, Twain connected with Charles Henry Webb, founder of the *Californian*, who had returned home east after an exodus out west. Webb and Twain visited the offices of publisher George Carleton at 499 Broadway. Carleton did not warmly welcome Twain, who was not dressed in the latest fashions. Unimpressed with Twain's pitch of combining "The Jumping Frog" with a collection of newspaper sketches, Carleton famously waved his hand across the room and remarked, "Books. Look at those shelves. Every one of them is loaded with books that are waiting for publication. Do I want any more? Excuse me, I don't." Regardless of the publisher's cold reception (which he would reportedly regret decades later), Webb believed in his friend and offered to publish his book. Twain, known to his friends as "Sam," agreed to take royalties of 10 percent.

Webb and Twain took a break from the proofing process and went back down to Broadway to meet with an old intimate of theirs from the Washoe,

Frank Fuller, secretary of Utah Territory from 1861 to 1863, who was now working in finance. They wanted to enlist Fuller in helping launch Twain's New York lecture tour. Although a lifelong friend of Twain, Fuller had the same evaluation Carleton did of the young journalist's wardrobe. "Mark was a very fine dresser and thought that his ordinary sack suit would be good enough to lecture in," Fuller recalled to the *New York Times*. "I told him he must wear evening dress, and he said he had never a worn a claw-hammer in his life. I put a first-class tailor on the job and made Mark get a suitable collar and necktie."

Appropriately dressed for the occasion, Twain made his New York debut at the Cooper Institute on May 6, 1867. A couple days later, the *New York Tribune* published a review, prefacing that the lecturer was already deserving of some notoriety as the author of "Joe Smiley and His Jumping Frog." Twain has been "immediately entered as a candidate for high position among writers of his class, and passages from his first contribution to the metropolitan press became proverbs in the mouths of admirers. No reputation was ever more rapidly won. The only doubt appeared to be whether he could satisfactorily sustain it." Twain did; with his writings, he now had a new medium to expand his reputation and influence. Speaking before a house "crowded beyond all exception," Twain was "deliberate and measured to the last degree" in his delivery as he lounged "comfortably around his platform, seldom referring to notes."

After delivering two other lectures in New York, but his book sales flat, Twain was restless. Writing to his mother and family on June 1, he let loose:

> *All I do know or feel is that I am wild with impatience to move—move—Move! Half a dozen times I have wished I had sailed long ago in some ship that wasn't going to keep me chained here to chafe for lagging ages while she got ready to go. Curse the endless delays! They always kill me—they make me neglect every duty & then I have a conscience that tears me like a wild beast. I wish I never had to stop anywhere a month. I do more mean things the moment I get a chance to fold my hands & sit down than ever I can get forgiveness for.*

Twain's restlessness was in part due to the delayed departure from New York of the *Quaker City*, a luxury cruise ship that was to take the first-of-its-kind whirlwind trip to the Holy Land, Europe and North Africa. Twain had arranged for his steerage, $1,200, to be paid by the editors of the *Alta California* in exchange for travel letters. (He would also write letters for the *New York Tribune*.) On June 8, the *Quaker City* departed New York. His experiences aboard the ship and on land would alter Twain's life in two ways: first, he would befriend Charles Langdon, whose sister, Olivia, Twain would eventually marry after a year's courtship; second, he would gather enough material through his correspondence to publish his first full-length book. However, before any of these life-altering events transpired, Twain made another move.

During a layover in Naples, Italy, Twain lost track of time and was up late at night, addressing his "folks" in a letter sent to Orion's law offices in St. Louis. "I wrote to Bill Stewart today accepting his private secretaryship in Washington next winter. When I come to think of it, I believe it can be made one of the best paying berths in Washington."

At thirty-two, Twain epitomized the footloose frontier spirit of the young nation—unformed, unsophisticated and underestimated but burning with ambition to realize a vast potential. Venturing fearlessly in pursuit of opportunity, from Missouri to the East to the raw greed of the Nevada silver mines to California and the remote Sandwich Islands, Twain found his dream along the way. Taking the sea voyage around to New York City, he began to realize that dream. By way of the Old World, now a proven journalist, he was on his way to the capital of the frontier nation, where he would alight briefly. It was a seminal, albeit short, stay before he would once again resume his peripatetic world wandering.

CHAPTER 3
The Scupper Nong Letter

The Scupper Nong Letters—From the National Capital—An Interview with General Grant. By Mark Twain.
—(Philadelphia) Daily Evening Telegraph, *November 30, 1867*

During research for this book, an article in the *New York Times* was discovered that has the evidential markings of Twain's Washington correspondence but has yet to be recognized and included in the accepted canon. The 1,700-word article is indicative of Twain for its humorous style as well as specific circumstances.* From the letter, which appeared on the front page of the *Times* on November 29, 1867, it appears that Twain, the nascent capital correspondent, literally hit the ground running upon landing in Washington. His prodigious output continued throughout his three-and-a-half-month stay in the city. Entitled "The Scupper Nong Letters—From the National Capital—An Interview with General Grant," the letter was the one and only time "Scupper Nong" had a byline for the *New York Times*. The next day, the *Evening Telegraph* in Philadelphia reprinted the article (as was customary with the nineteenth-century newspaper exchange system) inside the paper on page six, with one small addition. Tucked underneath the article's headline was "By Mark Twain."

---

*. This finding has yet to be presented for peer review among the well-established network of Twain scholars and researchers. In corresponding with experts in the field of Twain Studies during the summer of 2013, it is clear this discovery will warrant further investigation and a larger word count, with endnotes, than this chapter can support.

Twain, apparently writing as Nong, with an enlarged sense of self-importance, led off his letter by declaring, "I have not observed the announcement by any of the 'Specials' of my arrival in this political metropolis (which to my mind is rather a drink-opolis) as your occasional correspondent." He continued, "[T]hough unheralded, like many greater men, I did arrive on time." Upon reaching Washington, Nong took immediate action in fulfilling the role, as he understood it, of a capital correspondent: "Having read the papers pretty generally, considering my limited opportunities among your exchanges, I of course had learned enough to know that the first duty of any Washington correspondent, of whatever grade or rank, is to ascertain the views of the General of our armies on political matters." Before his "train whirled into the Baltimore [& Ohio] depot" on New Jersey Avenue at six o'clock in the morning, Nong knew where he was headed: General Grant's residence on Douglas Row, at the corner of New Jersey Avenue and I Street, "directly north of the depot and the Capitol," even though "[i]t was rather early in the morning, it is true, for a formal call, but business is ever before pleasure." Starting out from the depot at a brisk pace, "with satchel in hand, disguised in a patent paper shirt-bosom and cuffs," Nong was caught by surprise. Headed in the same direction were "six other correspondent-looking individuals like myself." Nong was not going to lose the story to lesser competition. "They walked fast, but I walked faster. It was evident that we instinctively understood each other. Directly we all broke into a run, and being somewhat given to running, I am free to say that your correspondent fairly distanced the others and made the first and only quarter in a very fair time."

Meeting a servant on the steps to the "mansion," Nong knew he had to act quickly and hurriedly asked if General Grant was up and accepting visitors. "He is just waking himself with his second cigar and looking to see what the *Chronicle* found out about him yesterday," the servant said, alluding to the recent coverage of Grant in John Forney's paper. Nong was ready with a reply and "assume[d] a Senatorial aspect," before stating, "Tell him that a gentleman who has always been a friend of his and of his father's first-cousin desires to see him on very special business." Nong was admitted into a private room "guarded by a miniature canon [*sic*] in each corner," which he guessed had been captured at the battle of Fort Donelson in Tennessee. By this time, the other correspondents had made it to the home and were permitted to enter, but they were shown to a separate room, provoking a chuckle from Nong.

After waiting an hour or so, General Grant finally appeared, "clad in full uniform, and had buckled on his sword from the sanitary fairs, to do honor to the occasion." As Grant entered the room, Nong rose and introduced himself as "Hon. Scupper Nong, late of New York, presenting my credentials from your office." Grant formally offered Nong a seat and reviewed his papers without offering a word. "I thought he did not seem very happy nor as cordial as an old friend could have wished," Nong wrote, attributing Grant's indifference to "the early hour and the possible lack of his morning coffee."

Finding nothing untoward in Nong's papers, Grant took his seat and looked at Nong "[a]s if to say, 'Well, what do you want?' though he actually said nothing. Whereupon [Nong] spoke. 'It is a fine morning.'" Unmoved by such a simple statement, Grant "merely glanced out of the window but sat pensively silent. He did not appear to be in his usual communicative mood." Nong felt his "ardor rather dampened." Niceties aside, Nong was here to score a headlining interview with General Grant and make his name among his fellow Washington correspondents.

After twisting his thumbs, crossing his feet and putting on his "most winning and fraternal expression," Nong "came sideways to the point." It was now or never:

> *Gen. Grant, the whole country, indeed I may say the world, is very anxious to know just what you think on the Reconstruction question and on politics generally. The nation is breathlessly waiting to hear you speak. Now, I am a friend of yours; I have no personal ends in view. I have always been a friend of your family. You may speak to me in perfect confidence…let me humbly suggest that you say something to relieve this immense pressure on the minds of men in general and of myself in particular. Just say one word, a single word. Do you sustain the President or do you stand by Congress?*

Still stoic, Grant "twitched nervously in his chair for a minute, pushed his hands down deep into his pockets, and looked as if he was absorbed in thought." The future president turned the line of questioning around on the cub correspondent: "Have you seen the Jeff Davis pony? I captured it at Vicksburg." Nong was determined to avoid any detours and persisted with his line of questioning. "General Grant, you needn't think to put off an old friend, who sincerely desires your welfare, with talking horse. I know nothing of horses. I have only my country (rolling my eyes lovingly to an American flag which hung over the mantel), my dear country in view—I may say I love it. I would have willingly died for it, only I had a small contract for furnishing blankets in the army which made my life dear to me and occupied all my

General Ulysses S. Grant and his horse, circa 1864. *Library of Congress.*

spare time during the late alienation of my brethren." Although Grant was not in the mood for talking, he was, Nong wrote, ready for a smoke or two. Grant reached into a side drawer of his desk and "took out a couple of very prominent Havanas." Nong thought the general would extend him one in a show of brotherhood and mutual love for country. The reporter was mistaken. Grant put "one in each corner of his expressive mouth [and] proceeded to light both at once with a single match and to puff away as he loved to smoke."

Nong's combative spirit was now "stirred" with Grant's increased evasions, and he "returned to the attack." Would the general not answer his questions explicitly? With a renewed show of force, Nong broke through to Grant. The correspondent wrote, "Then [Grant] knew his man, and turning around and looking at me as if I were General Lee, and we were settling terms of amicable adjustment, he responded as follows: 'Have you had your breakfast?'" Showing a military resolve, which Nong already admitted he didn't have, he stood his ground and replied, "Won't you trust me, General? Can't you confide in a friend who would fain be your bosom companion? I'll tell you all I know if you'll only ask me. Then answer my question." Pondering Nong's stubbornness, Grant continued "smoking still more vigorously; and after a painful silence of ten minutes, he spoke again." Grant asked the reporter if he had been in touch with the leading editors of the day, including John Forney and Francis Preston Blair Sr. When Nong said he hadn't spoken with any of them because "[t]hey know nothing," Grant contended, "Neither do I." At this, Grant grinned until one of the two cigars fell from his mouth, which he caught in stride.

His confidence undermined and feelings "wounded in the house of a friend," Nong was still determined and said, conscious to not speak in an overly imploring manner, "General Grant, do you not mean to tell me what you think? Reflect upon the wants of the people. They are all looking to you. The nation is waiting for your nod. Won't you speak? Speak one; speak for all." Grant had had enough of the interrogation and "very emphatically" said "no" before asking his servant to show the other correspondents in.

Suppressing his damaged ego, Nong was in the process of making one more appeal before Grant turned to him and "[s]miled on me so blandly, without ever removing either of the cigars, and said between his teeth as he bowed rather coldly and triumphantly, 'Won't you stop to breakfast, Mr. Scipio?'" Grant had confused Nong's alleged first name of Scupper with that of Scipio the Great, a Roman general who had defeated Hannibal in the Second Punic War. At this, the door opened and the other correspondents came "pouring in, nearly pushing" Nong over as he left. Back at his "room on the eighth floor of the Willard," Nong felt he was now "a better if not wiser man," although the interview had not gone as he would have wanted. "After reflecting upon the subject of my interview, I felt warranted in saying, and saying truthfully, that General Grant knows what he is about. And I think, I may add, that if anybody else knows what he knows, I don't see how they found it out. I may call again, but perhaps it would be as well as not. And so I leave it."

Deciding to explore Washington and his new environs, Nong left the Willard (which did not have eight floors in 1867) and went out to Pennsylvania Avenue, where, by coincidence, he met the other six correspondents just returned from their interview. In a postscript to his letter, Nong detailed his brief conversation: "All I could get from them was to this effect, that General Grant has gone to breakfast. I asked them what General Grant thought on the Reconstruction question. But a heavy draft of air passing that way just then fell upon them, as they seemed rather warm, and they all simultaneously sneezed, and I passed on."

Nong couldn't let it go, finishing off his solitary Washington letter by writing, "In conclusion, the more I think of it, the more I am convinced that General Grant's opinions are all right, and you may so announce to the country upon my authority. And you may say that I am fresh from an interview with him."

The discovery of the "Scupper Nong" letter coincides with a "bombshell revelation" first published in the 2012 edition of the *Mark Twain Journal* that deduces "exactly how and when Samuel Clemens reached a firm decision to adopt 'Mark Twain' as his pen name." Written by rare book collector and noted Twain researcher Kevin Mac Donnell, the article presents convincing evidence that the origins of the most famous *nom de plume* in all of American letters derives from "an anonymous comic sketch making fun of southerners at a nautical convention debating what to do about the very serious problem of their compasses always pointing north" that appeared in the "foremost comic magazine of its era," *Vanity Fair*, on January 26, 1861. The burlesque sketch is, according to Mac Donnell, the first known use of "Mark Twain" in print as a proper name. In the sketch, five angry mariners debate: "Mr. Pine Knott," "Mr. Lee Scupper," "Mr. Pine Knott," "Mr. Raitlin" and "Mr. Mark Twain." Mac Donnell discusses the provenance of the name Lee Scupper: "Since the fifteenth century, this term has been applied to the drain-holes spaced along the outer edges of the deck of a sailing vessel through which water could drain harmlessly back to sea. Decks on nineteenth-century sailing vessels could get dirty, and if a strong wind was blowing across the deck, the leeward scuppers are where the grime and sewage on the decks would be driven out (or often clog). It also implies that those downwind scuppers are many points off the windward side—as if to imply somebody not quite at full sail in a strong wind. After a battle, it was common to describe scuppers as running with blood. The name was not complimentary." It is within reason that when Twain, former Mississippi river boat pilot and experienced ocean traveler, arrived in Washington, he still recalled this *Vanity Fair* sketch that used the nautical term he would subsequently adopt as his most used pen name.

But where does "Nong" come from? From various accounts, it appears to be a slang term for an idiot. As a young man of thirty-two, Twain was known to use slang in private and public. Writing from Washington City in late January 1868, Twain confided, "It seems I have been using slang again. I am so unfortunate. I know I never, never, never shall get reformed up to the regulation standard. Every time I reform in one direction, I go overboard in another. Now, once & for all, I will not use any more slang. But I suppose I shall make some other blunder that is just as bad & get into trouble again." The day before, writing to Mary Fairbanks in response to her concerns over the slang that was printed in the papers transcribing his speech at a banquet for the Washington Newspaper Correspondents' Club, Twain promised, "I will rigidly eschew slang & vulgarity in future, even in foolish dinner speeches, when on my guard." That Twain, at this time, was familiar with the term "scupper" and used slang is beyond question.

There are other similarities between Twain and "Scupper Nong." Both had recently arrived in Washington from New York, both were familiar with the Willard, both were "occasional" correspondents and both were ambitious. Just days before the Scupper Nong letter appeared, Twain, after speaking with James Rankin Young, Washington bureau chief of the *New York Tribune*, wrote John Russell Young, editor of the *Tribune*, informing him of a potential conflict: "I have neglected until this last moment (5 pm) to write you that Mr. Bennett Jr. offers me an occasional correspondence with the Herald—impersonal, of course, I suppose. I spoke to your brother—he said I had better write you. I wish to remain on the Tribune, with signature—on the Herald without, will not make any difference will it?" No known letters exist detailing a potential offer Twain received from or proposed to the *New York Times* to file "occasional" letters from Washington, but it is hard to imagine Twain would have passed up an opportunity to contribute. The absence of a clipping of the Scupper Nong letter from Twain's Washington scrapbook, which he still flipped through in his seventies, cannot be overlooked, but is likely due to the fact that Twain wanted the article to remain obscure, unnoticed and hidden. The publication of the Scupper Nong letter, which he pulled off rather undetected, surely gave Twain an internal, if not external, juice as he hit the Washington City beat. Twain could handle this town.

One of the most revealing characteristics of the Scupper Nong letter is its similarity to Twain's well-known article "Concerning Gen. Grant's Intentions," which was published in the *Tribune* in December 1868. Writing from Washington, Twain "had been up trying to get at Gen. Grant's opinion and intentions concerning certain matters and had found him, in a manner, speechless." Alternating between no response and the phrase "Let us have Peace!" General Grant's disposition toward

View inside an office of a New York newspaper in Washington, *Harper's New Monthly Magazine*, 1881. *Author's collection.*

Twain, as described in his December 1868 newspaper article, is a seeming continuation of the Scupper Nong letter. As prominent Twain scholar Louis J. Budd wrote in *Mark Twain: Social Philosopher*, "In the stance of court jester, he used safe targets…or if he used important people, as when 'Concerning General Grant's Intentions' spoofed that budding candidate's taciturnity, he felt his way with caution. Still, he could not be too timid whom he criticized if he wanted to keep up the demand for his material."

Lastly, when General Grant bids "Scupper Nong" a farewell, he erroneously addresses him as "Mr. Scipio." As a West Point graduate, Grant was surely familiar with the Roman general who defeated Hannibal, so it was an understandable fictitious slip of the tongue. For Twain, Scipio had another meaning that was connected to his childhood. In 1902, when Twain made a return visit to Hannibal, he rode around with a boyhood friend and a local reporter. Riding along the Mississippi River, the cadre headed toward "old Scipio" which, unlike Hannibal, never flourished as a port city in Marion County, Missouri. Twain and his friend told the reporter for the *Ralls County Record*, "Scipio was to be a great city and defeat Hannibal, repeating the history of the old Roman and Carthaginian days, but the order was reversed, and today Hannibal is the victor and Scipio is only a memory." In Washington City in the winter of 1867–68, Twain had not yet become synonymous in the public realm with stories of his mythologized boyhood spent along the Mississippi River, but they were always at the back of his mind, waiting to be used.

CHAPTER 4
The Washington Syndicate

*Here is a Macedonian cry projected towards you out of the old
Bohemian Washington days.*
—William Swinton to Samuel Clemens, August 16, 1883

W hen Mark Twain, taking the train from New York, disembarked at
Washington in the early morning hours of November 22, 1867,
no one was there to meet him. His name and fame had slowly emerged
in recent years; within the calendar year, he had become a self-propelled
starburst with the publication of his first book, a string of successful New
York lectures and an ongoing series of special travel correspondence for
the *New York Tribune*. Politics was the perfect fuel to feed Twain's sense of
satire. This city would be catalytic to the rise of the most prominent man
in American letters. During his short stay in Washington City, Twain
published more than two dozen attributed local and national articles for
the *Evening Star* (one), *Daily Morning Chronicle* (one), the *Daily Alta California*
(eight), the Virginia City *Territorial Enterprise* (eleven), the *Chicago Republican*
(three), the *New York Herald* (three), the *New York Tribune* (three) and the
New York Citizen (one). He also made his first contribution to *The Galaxy*, a
literary magazine based in New York. His articles were not insignificant
blurbs; they were instructive and substantive, usually upwards of 1,500
words covering the daily tension and maneuvering between Congress and
President Andrew Johnson, the contortions of various lobby interests,
local Washington and the unique social structure and mores of the ruling

Samuel Clemens, known by his *nom de plume* Mark Twain, circa 1867. *Library of Congress.*

political class. These Washington writings and his experiences in the legislative metropolis would later form the foundation for his first novel, *The Gilded Age: A Tale of Today*, co-authored with Charles Dudley Warner.

During his time in the city, Twain was at a turning point in his life. He was still mainly a journalist, not yet a fully developed author with original work to his credit. While in Washington, he was offered a chance at authorship from Elisha Bliss of the American Publishing Company and commenced work immediately. His drive to tackle his first complete and full-fledged book was ignited while in Washington. Twain was a literary powder keg ready to explode upon the world. In Washington, the match was lit to spark the fuse. Before the fire was lit underneath him, Twain ran petty schemes simply to get a drink for him and his partner.

Decades after leaving the bohemian life of Washington behind him, Mark Twain, the author, was prone to reminisce about his time and adventures in the capital city. On at least four occasions he mentioned (each time his memory offering slightly different details) a failed scheme to form a newspaper syndicate with William Swinton, a former Civil War correspondent for the *New York Times* and emerging author at the time. By Twain's admission, during his stay in Washington he moved a minimum of five times after first rooming with Nevada senator William Stewart. During his repeated inter-city travels, he shared lodgings with a roll call of prominent correspondents, including John Henry Riley, Hiram J. Ramsdell, George Adams, George Alfred Townsend, Jerome Stillson and Swinton. On a visit to Washington in the spring of 1889, Twain recalled his younger days as a capital correspondent to a journalist with the *New York Herald*. "I was rather new and shy, and I did not mingle in the festivities of Newspaper Row." The "Row" was a number of offices or news bureaus located along

14th Street across from the Willard Hotel. According to Ben Perley Poore, "The Washington offices of the more important newspapers in distant cities have each its suit of apartments, comprising anteroom, reading-room, and reporters' room, beyond which is the carefully guarded 'sanctum sanctorum' of the chief correspondent, with a trusty janitor as his body-guard." Twain and Swinton were off the Row, not among the gang of correspondents who would gather and populate the street and fill the bureau's offices. "From nine o'clock in the evening until after midnight unless there is a night session at the Capitol, Newspaper Row is a busy place," Poore wrote in *Harper's Magazine*. "Each correspondent is on the alert, anxious not to be 'beaten' by some rival, who has perhaps been more fortunate than himself in obtaining information. Some whose respective journals are in different localities exchange their items, while others," such as Twain, "when deficient in news, do not hesitate to manufacture it." The special correspondents, like Twain, Poore recognized were adroit at "concocting their nocturnal budgets."

"Impeachment—Scene in 'Newspaper Row,' Washington on the Night After the Vote—Sketched by T.R. Davis." *Harper's Weekly*, May 20, 1868. By the time this print ran, Twain was in San Francisco finishing his manuscript for *The Innocents Abroad. DC Public Library, Washingtoniana Division*.

These special capital correspondents did not usually mingle among the Row. "A few correspondents are located elsewhere," Poore acknowledged, "and some of them, who represent half a dozen or more journals, find it difficult to secure room on the exterior walls of their modest quarters for the pretentious signs which have been sent to them by their different employers, each one of whom boasts in his paper of 'our own correspondent,' although he only pays for a small fraction of that individual's services." These were the members of the "press corps who will correspond with any paper, any where, of any politics, for a pittance."

While moonlighting as private secretary to Senator Stewart, Twain wrote Washington letters for nearly half a dozen papers from San Francisco to Chicago to New York. Although rather reticent in retrospect, Twain was conspicuous around Washington during the winter of 1867–68. He delivered lectures to overflowing crowds, attended receptions and closely associated with the city's flood of newspapermen and women who had settled in Washington during and immediately after the Civil War and who were now pondering other literary pursuits. As Donald Ritchie writes in his authoritative work, *Press Gallery: Congress and the Washington Correspondents*, "By war's end, the swelled ranks of newspaper correspondents settled permanently into Washington, considerably expanding the band of prewar letter writers. Every editor of a major daily, and many minor ones as well, wanted his own 'special correspondent' at the capital. Those who covered the war lingered to cover the political battles and watched the generals they had followed in the fields take seats in the chambers below them." Always on the hunt for a quick dollar, Twain sought to take advantage where others hadn't before.

"A little later that winter, William Swinton and I housed together," Twain told the *Herald* reporter as he "strayed into the press gallery, threw back his overcoat, adjusted his gold spectacle on his nose and looked around." According to Twain, "Swinton invented the idea—at least it was new to me—of manifolding correspondence, I mean of sending duplicates of a letter to various widely separated newspapers. We projected an extensive business, but for some reason or other, we took it out in dreaming—never really tried it." Twain would retell a version of this same story at least three more times over the next two decades.

William Swinton

In an address before the Brooklyn Press Club on December 10, 1892, William C. De Witt, who had helped frame the original draft of Brooklyn's municipal charter, commemorated the life of his friend William Swinton. In his opening remarks, De Witt proclaimed, "You are the guild of letters. It is yours to maintain the sovereignty of the mind and the aristocracy of genius. And you may rest assured that with whatsoever vanity or pride, power or splendor, any other domination may have intrenched [sic] itself about you, the source of all real individual merit and of all true national progress lies in the intellectual forces, in the service of which be you ever, like the knights errant of old, proud, chivalric, indomitable, triumphant!"

In his era, Swinton was a literary iconoclast. Born "of a religious brood" in Scotland in 1833, Swinton entered Amherst College in Massachusetts, where he studied to be a minister. However, he started his career as a scholar and professor at Edgeworth Seminary in Greensboro, North Carolina, before joining the faculty at Mount Washington Collegiate Institute in New York City in the late 1850s. While there, he contributed essays and reviews to *Putnam's* and *Atlantic Monthly* while writing a book on etymology, *Rambles Among Words: Their Poetry, History, and Wisdom*, to which Walt Whitman contributed. At the outbreak of the Civil War, Swinton approached his friend Henry J. Raymond about his desire to chronicle the Army of the Potomac and was made a war correspondent for the *New York Times*, later turning his experiences into two popular books: *The Campaigns of the Army of the Potomac* and *The Twelve Decisive Battles of the Civil War*. As a war correspondent, Swinton achieved a certain infamy.

In his memoirs, Ulysses S. Grant tells of meeting Swinton, who was presented to him "as a literary gentleman who wished to accompany the army with a view of writing the history of the war when it was over." Grant was assured by Swinton that "he was not present as a correspondent of the press." After the first few days of fighting "in the Wilderness," General Meade came to Grant's "tent for consultation, bringing with him some of his staff officers. Both his staff and mine retired to the camp-fire some yards in front of the tent, thinking our conversation should be private," Grant recalled. "There was a stump a little to one side, and between the front of the tent and camp-fire. One of my staff, Colonel T.S. Bowers, saw what he took to be a man seated on the ground and leaning against the stump, listening to the conversation between Meade and myself. [He] called the attention of Colonel Rowley to it, and the latter immediately took the man

General Ambrose Burnside reviewing a newspaper alongside his staff and Mathew Brady. Burnside ordered William Swinton shot. *Library of Congress.*

by the shoulder and asked him, in language more forcible than polite, what he was doing there." The man "proved to be Swinton, the 'historian,' and his replies to the question were evasive and unsatisfactory, and he was warned against further eavesdropping." That was not the last Grant would hear of Swinton. At Cold Harbor, General Meade came to Grant's headquarters with the message that "General Burnside had arrested Swinton, who at some previous time had given great offence, and had ordered him to be shot that afternoon. I promptly ordered the prisoner to be released but…expelled from the lines of the army, not to return again on pain of punishment."

Following the war, Swinton settled in Washington, where according to De Witt, *The Twelve Decisive Battles of the Civil War* was partly composed. In his Washington letter to the *Daily Alta California* dated December 17, 1867, and published January 28, 1868, Twain wrote that A.D. Richardson's book *The Mississippi and Beyond*, published by the American Publishing Company (which was also seeking a title from Twain), and Swinton's book were "the most saleable books, I believe, that have issued from the press this year."

"I first made his acquaintance at the bar of Willard's Hotel, in Washington, during the trial of President Johnson under the impeachment of the House of Representatives. Both of us were warm friends of the President and engaged in efforts to thwart and defeat his enemies," De Witt recalled. Swinton then made another career pivot, heading west to become the "chair of Belles-Lettres at the University of California." Although removed by the Board of Regents in 1874, Swinton had begun authoring textbooks on literature, history and geography, which would become his vocation for the next eighteen years. De Witt eulogized that Swinton "had done more for the cause of education as an author of the text books of our schools than any other American." In all, Swinton wrote more than a dozen titles that can still be found in Washington-area used bookstores.

TWAIN AND SWINTON'S ADVENTURES

In chapter twenty-five of Twain's autobiographical musings, published in the *North American Review* in December 1907, Twain "altered" Swinton's last name but told nearly the exact same story he had first mentioned in 1889:

> *I had just come back from the Quaker City Excursion and had made a contract with Bliss of Hartford to write "The Innocents Abroad." I was out of money, and I went down to Washington to see if I could earn enough there to keep me in bread and butter while I should write the book. I came across William Clinton, [a]nd together we invented a scheme for our mutual sustenance; we became the fathers and originators of what is a common feature in the newspaper world now—the syndicate. We became the old original first Newspaper Syndicate on the planet; it was on a small scale, but that is usual with untried new enterprises. We had twelve journals on our list; they were all weeklies, all obscure and poor and all scattered far away among the back settlements. It was a proud thing for those little newspapers to have a Washington correspondence, and a fortunate thing for us that they felt in that way about it. Each of the twelve took two letters a week from us, at a dollar per letter; each of us wrote one letter per week and sent off six duplicates of it to these benefactors, thus acquiring twenty-four dollars a week to live on—which was all we needed in our cheap and humble quarters.*

According to Edgar M. Branch, distinguished Twain scholar, some of the articles "probably designed to appear in the 'syndicate' of weeklies" were "General Spinner as a Religious Enthusiast," "Mr. Brown, the Sergeant-at-Arms of the Senate" and "Interview with Gen. Grant." These articles have not yet been published, although there is evidence from the June 1868 *Harper's Magazine* that "General Spinner as a Religious Enthusiast" was published.

When was this Washington syndicate between Swinton and Twain conceived? It is unclear, yet from Twain's letter to John Russell Young, editor of the *New York Tribune*, on December 4, 1867, the two budding literary men were already hanging tough. "I thought Swinton was going up today, but he has put it off," Twain wrote as his first line in a letter explaining to Young that he had just received a publishing "proposition" and might need to repossess the "three Holy Land letters I sent up." Swinton is next mentioned in a letter Twain sent to his family on January 20, 1868. Sharing his desire to secure an interview with General Grant, Twain disclosed his plan: "Swinton & I are going to get the old man into a private room at Willard's & start his tongue with a whisky punch." From references to Swinton in his personal letters at the time, and Twain's subsequent memories of Swinton, it is apparent that the two men established an intimate bond during their Washington days that they both remembered fondly throughout their lives.

Not everyone was so warm to Swinton. In George Alfred Townsend's unpublished memoirs, he reveals that he was also approached by Swinton to form a Washington syndicate. On page four of Townsend's unpublished manuscript, entitled "War Correspondents' Arch," he recalls, "William Swinton was a Scotch schoolteacher of irregular habits and dubious American patriotism, with considerable of the military critic. He wrote the history of the Army of the Potomac in a way to flatter and delight Lee's army, followed by the 'Decisive Battles,' which reaffirmed his Levite view of his comrades, gravitated into a school book writer and ended without context. He and I once planned a bureau of political correspondence from Washington, which, happily, I was spared."

In a January 1906 auto-dictation published in 2010, Twain remembered Swinton again:

> *I had come back from the Quaker City Excursion. I had gone to Washington to write "The Innocents Abroad," but before beginning that book it was necessary to earn some money to live on meantime, or borrow it—which would be difficult—or take it where it reposed, unwatched—which would be unlikely. So I started the first Newspaper Correspondence Syndicate that an unhappy world ever saw. I started it in conjunction with William Swinton, a brother of the*

admirable John Swinton [editorialist for the *New York Times*]. *William
Swinton was a brilliant creature, highly educated and accomplished. He was
such a contrast to me that I did not know which of us most to admire, because
both ends of a contrast are equally delightful to me.*

While a "splendid literature charm[ed]" Twain and Swinton, they were also
enchanted by alcohol at the time. "Swinton kept a jug," Twain remembered.
"It was sometimes full but seldom as full as himself—and it was when he was
fullest that he was most competent with his pen. We wrote a letter apiece once
a week and copied them and sent them to twelve newspapers, charging each of
the newspapers a dollar apiece. And although we didn't get rich, it kept the jug
going and partly fed the two of us." "[Twenty-four dollars a week] would have
really been riches to us," Twain wrote in the *North American Review* in 1907, "if we
hadn't had to support that jug; because of the jug, we were always sailing pretty
close to the wind and any tardiness in the arrival of any part of income was sure
to cause us some inconvenience." A shortage occurred, and "we had to have
three dollars, and we had to have it before the close of the day." Swinton directed
Twain "to go out and find it" while he said he would do the same. "[Swinton]
didn't seem to have any doubt that we would succeed, but I knew that that was
his religion working in him; I hadn't the same confidence. I hadn't any idea of
where to turn to raise all that bullion, and I said so." Twain inferred that Swinton
was ashamed of him "because of my weak faith. He told me to give myself no
uneasiness, no concern; and said in a simple, confident, and unquestioning way,
'the Lord will provide.'" Twain "wandered around the streets for an hour, trying
to think up some way to get that money, but nothing suggested itself."

Twain took a break at the Ebbitt House, where "a dog came loafing along.
He paused, glanced up at me and said with his eyes, 'Are you friendly?'" Twain
answered with his eyes that he was. The dog wagged its tail and advanced to
Twain, resting its "jaw on my knee and lift[ing] his brown eyes to my face in a
winningly affectionate way." Twain "stroked his smooth brown head and fondled
his drooping ears, and we were a pair of lovers right away." In the next moment,
Brigadier General Nelson A. Miles, "the hero of the land, came strolling by
in his blue and gold splendors, with everybody's admiring gaze upon him."
General Miles saw the dog, and a "light in his eye" showed that he "had a warm
place in his heart for dogs like this gracious creature; then he came forward and
patted the dog." The general asked if the dog was for sale.

"I was greatly moved," Twain recalled. "It seemed a marvelous thing to me
the way [Swinton's] prediction had come true." The general asked the price,
to which Twain responded three dollars. Although the general offered to pay

more, Twain was steadfast in asking only three dollars. Getting what he thought was a bargain, the general handed Twain the money and "led the dog away and disappeared upstairs." Pleased at how Providence had come through, Twain sat there in his small-time victory, unmoved. "In about ten minutes, a gentle-faced middle-aged gentleman came along and began to look around here and there and under tables and everywhere." Twain asked if the man was looking for a dog. "His face was sad, before, and troubled; but it lit up gladly now." Twain had seen the dog and the gentleman whom the dog had followed, he confessed, without implicating himself in the disappearance. Twain offered to help find the canine.

"I have seldom seen a person look so grateful—and there was gratitude in his voice, too, when he conceded that he would like me to try. I said I would do it with great pleasure but that as it might take a little time, I hoped he would not mind paying me something for my trouble." Payment would be no problem, the man said, and he then asked how much. Twain replied, "Three dollars." The man offered to pay ten dollars, but Twain declined. "No, three is the price," he said, starting for the stairs "without waiting further argument, for [Swinton] had said that that was the amount the Lord would provide, and it seemed to me that it would be sacrilegious to take a penny more than was promised." Twain obtained the general's room number from a clerk, and "when I reached the room, I found the General there caressing his dog, and quite happy." To the general's vexation, Twain said he needed the dog back. "Take him again?" General Miles asked. "Why, he is my dog; you sold him to me—and at your own price." That all was true, Twain agreed. "[B]ut I have him because the man wants him again." "What man?" the general asked. "The man that owns him; he wasn't my dog," Twain admitted. After a brief argument, Twain "paid back the three dollars and led the dog down-stairs, passed him over to his owner and collected three for my trouble." Twain "went away with a good conscience, because I had acted honorably; I never could have used the three that I sold the dog for because it was not rightly my own. But the three I got for restoring him to his rightful owner was righteously and properly mine because I had earned it. That man might never have gotten the dog back at all if it hadn't been for me."

Nearly forty years later, Twain met General Miles, "and he commented on the fact that we had known each other thirty years. He said it was strange that we had not met years before when we had both been in Washington. At that point, I changed the subject, and I changed it with art. The General seemed not to remember my part in that adventure, and I never had the heart to tell him about it."

CHAPTER 5
City Reporter

*I believe the Prince of Darkness could start a branch of hell in the District of
Columbia (if he has not already done it).*
—Mark Twain

An analysis of Mark Twain's writing as a capital correspondent reveals
that alongside his political jottings, he included local Washington in his
reportorial focus. In Virginia City and San Francisco, he had been a local
editor covering all matter of events from drab city agency meetings to the
theater to schools to the courthouse and corruption. Before Mark Twain
became known as a definitive American novelist, he was a local beat writer.
While in Washington, he continued to comment with flair and irony on local
affairs, although his audiences were in Midwest and Pacific locales. Many
decades ago, David C. Mearns compiled a bound, oversized file of Twain's
Washington clippings; reviewing the portfolio in the Manuscript Division of
the Library of Congress is to take a look back at a volatile Washington City
where cows freely roamed the streets and crime was plentiful.

Two days before the *Evening Star* announced Mark Twain's arrival in
Washington for the winter, its "Local News" section led with a small story,
"No Cow Allowed About the City Hall." Mayor Richard Wallach, appointed
by Lincoln in 1861 and subsequently elected by popular vote three times,
"complained of Washington Rollins, Catherine Madison, Patrick Foley,
Sarah E. Cook, and Mary Carroll, as allowing their cows to trespass upon the
lot in the rear of the City Hall." The violators were "arraigned before Justice

LOCAL NEWS.

NO COW ALLOWED ABOUT THE CITY HALL.—
Mayor Wallach yesterday complained of
Washington Rollins, Catherine Madison, Patrick Foley, Sarah E. Cook, and Mary Carroll,
as allowing their cows to trespass upon the
lot in the rear of the City Hall. They were
arraigned before Justice Walter, who fined
each $5 and $1 costs. Sarah E. Cook, who had
three cows, was required to pay $18.

"Local News," *Evening Star*, November 25, 1867. *DC Public Library, Washingtoniana Division.*

Walter, who fined each $5 and $1 costs. Sarah E. Cook, who had three cows, was required to pay $18." From annual reports of the city poundmaster to Congress in the decade following the Civil War, the existence of wayward hogs, goats, chickens, dogs and cows was not a laughing matter to property owners, who petitioned the city to get a lasso on the problem.

In an otherwise forgotten article, Twain satirized this dynamic of Washington City, which in his estimation appeared to be an urban barnyard with delinquent animals on the loose. Twain lampooned Washington in his February 19, 1868 column, "More Washington Morals," dated January 12, in the *Daily Alta California*:

> On New Year's morning, while Mr. George Worley's front door was standing open, a cow marched into the house—a cow that was out making her annual calls, I suppose—and before she was discovered had eaten up everything on the New Year's table in the parlor! Mr. Worley was not acquainted with the cow, never saw her before, and is at a loss to account for the honor of her visit. What do you think of a town where cows make New Year's calls? It may be the correct thing, but it has not been so regarded in the circles in which I have been accustomed to move. Morals are at a low stage in Washington, beyond question.

Was this veiled political and social commentary making the point that everyone in Washington, even the cows, was on the search for a meal ticket? Unlikely. This small sketch simply demonstrates that Twain was in touch with the city he covered. He was still a local reporter, capable of finding the humor in daily life wherever he was. Although not "accustomed to move" in cities where cows, valuable livestock, roamed free, he accepted that this was a part of Washington and immortalized one unknown cow, even if the story is apocryphal. On a more serious note, Twain reported on city crime, of which "[t]here is plenty." He could draw no humor from two "peculiar" cases he featured in his January 12 dispatch to the *Alta*, which ran just before his story on the ravenous city cow. No newcomer to carrying a pistol, hearing gunshots fired while composing late-night copy and reporting on police corruption and murder while in Nevada and California, Twain thought these two crimes worth noting without exaggeration. "Night before last a negro man collided with a white man in the street; the negro apologized, but the white man would not be appeased and grew abusive, and finally stabbed the negro [in] the heart."

The other specific crime Twain took note of generated public outcry across the city. As he reported:

> *Yesterday in open Court, while Judge [Abram B.] Olin was sentencing a man named McCauley, the latter sprang at the principal witness, a boy twelve years old, and made a savage lunge at his breast with a knife. The Judge remanded him at once, of course, to be cited before the Grand Jury. What is your general opinion of the morals of the Capital now? When people get to attempting murder in the Courts of law, it is time to quit abusing Congress. Congress is bad enough, but it has not arrived at such depravity as this. This man who attempted the murder is not in any way connected with Congress. The fact is in every way creditable to that body. I do not deny that I am fond of abusing Congress, but when I get an opportunity like this to compliment them, I am only too happy to do it.*

On January 13, the *Daily Chronicle*'s lead editorial focused on "The Recent Attempt at Murder in Open Court." "The prisoner McCauley, who attempted to murder the boy, Thos. Kinley, in the court-room for testifying against him on Friday last is at present in his old quarter at the jail heavily ironed but still evinces a most revengeful spirit toward his would-be victim." The *Chronicle* laid out the facts it had gathered: "On the way to the jail, he stated that he had friends in the court-room who had agreed to kill the boy. He said also that the knife with which he attempted to kill the boy was given to him in the court-house by a colored boy, and if the judge had given him a

"Mark Twain in Washington," *Daily Alta California*, February 11, 1868. *University of California, Riverside.*

light sentence he would have taken it quietly, but as the repentance was of a severe one he intended to kill Kinley at the risk of his life."

Twain also reported on the mundane. The following appeared under "Miscellaneous" in a late-December dispatch to the *Daily Alta*: "By the report of the Superintendent of Colored Schools for the cities of Washington and Georgetown, it appears that there are, in all, 55 free colored schools, 57 teachers, 2,748 pupils—average attendance, daily, 2,500." For the *Territorial Enterprise*, he recorded the "general opinion" of a landlady who was unhappy with not only the congressman who skipped out on her but also "the false weights [that] were used in the market, the grocery stores, the butcher shops and all such places." According to the landlady, "The meat a butcher sells you for seven pounds can never [be] persuaded to weigh more than five and a half in your kitchen scales at home; a grocer's pound of butter usually weighs only three-quarters in scales that are unconscious and have no motive to deceive. They paint rocks and add them to your coal; they put sand in your sugar; lime in your flour; water in your milk; turpentine in your whisky; clothespins in your sausages; turnips in your canned peaches; they will rather cheat you out of ten cents than make a dollar out of you by honest dealing." Foreshadowing the theme of Twain's first novel, *The Gilded Age*, which was still years away, he concluded that Washington was built on the swindle from the halls of Congress to the storefronts of local merchants.

"What little I have seen of Washington in the short time I have been here leads me to think it must be correct."

Twain also made an effort to forecast local meteorology, commenting on Washington's "Scurrilous Weather" patterns, which any school-aged person in the Washington metropolitan area can appreciate. Writing in his introductory Washington letter for the *Territorial Enterprise*, Twain took issue with the city's uncertain weather: "I have been here a matter of ten days, but I do not know much about the place yet. There is too much weather. There is too much of it, and yet that is not the principal trouble. It is the quality rather than the quantity of it that I complain of; and more than against its quantity and its quality combined am I embittered against its character. It is tricky, it is changeable, and it is to the last degree unreliable." Caught in a blizzard during his first "flying trip" to Washington in 1854, Twain's consternation had not changed. The fickleness of the weather, he observed, mirrored the political atmosphere:

> *As politics go, so goes the weather. It trims to suit every phase of sentiment and is always ready. To-day it is a Democrat, to-morrow a Radical, the next day neither one thing nor the other. If a Johnson man goes over to the other side, it rains; if a Radical deserts to the Administration, it snows; if New York goes Democratic, it blows—naturally enough; if Grant expresses an opinion between two whiffs of smoke, it spits a little sleet uneasily; if all is quiet on the Potomac of politics, one sees only the soft haze of Indian summer from the Capitol windows; if the President is quiet, the sun comes out; if he touches the tender gold market, it turns up cold and freezes out the speculators; if he hints at foreign troubles, it hails; if he threatens Congress, it thunders; if treason and impeachment are broached, lo, there is an earthquake! If you are posted on politics, you are posted on the weather. I cannot manage either; when I go out with an umbrella, the sun shines; if I go without it, it rains; if I have my overcoat with me, I am bound to roast—if I haven't, I am bound to freeze. Some people like Washington weather. I don't. Some people admire mixed weather. I prefer to take mine "straight."*

With the Washington Monument still unfinished, Twain returned to another element of his 1854 Washington letter. As a teenager, Twain viewed the city from the perspective of an amateur "architecture critic," writing, "The Washington Monument is as yet but a plain white marble obelisk 150 feet high. It will no doubt be very beautiful when finished. When completed, an iron staircase will run up within 25 feet of the top. It is to be 550 feet high." Deliberate or not, he embraced the role of a preservation activist advocating a public-private partnership that could help finish the monument in "four years." More than a dozen years later, little work had been done. It was now, in Twain's eyes, an "ungainly old chimney of no earthly use to anybody" and "certainly is not in the least ornamental." Using nearly the same text to describe the yet-unfinished Washington Monument in *The Gilded Age*, written in 1873, Twain described the edifice in January 1868 as "[t]he general size and shape, and possesses about the dignity, of a sugar-mill chimney. It may suit the departed George Washington—I don't know. He may think it is pretty. It may be a comfort to him to look at it out of the clouds. He may enjoy perching on it to look around upon the scene of his earthly greatness, but it is not likely. It is not likely that any spirit would be so taken with that lumbering thing as to want to roost there. It is an eyesore to the people. It ought to be either pulled down or built up and finished."

In December 1884, the capstone was finally crowned on the monument, nearly four decades after the cornerstone was laid in 1848. The monument was dedicated to the public in February 1885, the same month that *Adventures of Huckleberry Finn* was published in the United States.

CHAPTER 6
A Literary Proposition

The Jumping Frog. By Mark Twain. $1.50.
—Daily Chronicle, *February 18, 1868*

A s it is, I don't think I will accomplish anything but my correspondence,"
Twain confided in a cover letter on November 25, 1867, to his friend
and first publisher, Charles Henry Webb. Twain had enclosed a copy of
a play he had drafted. Working "as an 'occasional' on the Tribune staff,"
having received a "letter from the Herald offering me the same position"
and the necessity of maintaining "up a Pacific coast correspondence," Twain
was "for business now," as he told his family in a letter written the same day.
However, unbeknownst to Twain, a book-publishing offer from Elisha Bliss
Jr. of the American Publishing Company of Hartford, Connecticut, who
had read Twain's "letters from the past," awaited his "reply at once." Sent
to Twain in care of the New York office of the *Tribune* and dated November
21, Bliss wrote, "We are perhaps the oldest subscription house in the country
and have never failed to give a book an immense circulation." Given the
lackluster sales of *The Jumping Frog*, published in May by Webb, this was
a step toward literary recognition for Twain. "If you have any thought of
writing a book, or could be induced to do so, we should be pleased to see
you, and will do so." Twain sat unaware in Washington for ten days before
the "letter was forwarded to the Tribune bureau in Washington."

After finally receiving the letter, Twain responded in full on December 2.
Twain had written "fifty-two letters for the San Francisco Alta California

Charles Henry Webb, original publisher of *The Jumping Frog*, visited Twain while in Washington City. *Author's collection*.

during the Quaker City excursion, about half of which have been printed thus far." Due to the *Alta*'s limited newspaper exchanges on the East Coast, it was unlikely "any of these letters have been copied on this side of the Rocky Mountains." Twain reported he had "other propositions for a book, but have doubted the propriety of interfering with good newspaper engagements except my way as an author could be demonstrated to be plain before me." According to Paine, "The exchange of those letters [between Twain and Bliss] marked the beginning of one of the most notable publishing connections in American literary history."

When, how and where Twain began writing what would become *The Innocents Abroad* is not exactly clear. From anecdotal accounts, Twain commenced work while in Washington before leaving in early March 1868 for San Francisco, where he would negotiate the release rights for the *Alta* letters. According to Stewart's account in his 1908 autobiography, when Twain arrived at 224 F Street NW, Washington, he was already in possession of his newfound publishing intention. "I have a proposition," Twain said. "There's millions in it. All I need is a little cash stake. I have been to the Holy Land with a party of innocent and estimable people who are fairly aching to be written up, and I think I could do the job neatly and with dispatch if I were not troubled with other, more pressing considerations. I've started the book already, and it is a wonder. I can vouch for it." Stewart asked to see the manuscript, and Twain obliged. "He pulled a dozen sheets or so from his pocket," Stewart remembered, "and handed them to me. I read what he had written and saw that it was bully, so I continued, 'I'll appoint you my clerk at the Senate, and you can live on the salary. There's a little hall bedroom across the way where you can sleep, and you can write your book in here. Help yourself to the whiskey and cigars, and wade in.'" That Twain did, staying up late into the night, to the disapproval of the landlord; Twain eventually earned a discharge from 224 F Street NW.

From an account published in the *Philadelphia Press* in 1883 by Hiram J. Ramsdell, Twain was actively writing his manuscript at a boardinghouse on Indiana Avenue NW. With an irreverent tone, Ramsdell called to mind that "at the time [George Alfred] Townsend, [Jerome] Stillson, [John Henry] Riley and myself never thought that Twain's book would amount to anything, and probably, he did not think it would either, but he was writing for the money his naked MS would bring him from his Hartford publisher. He needed that money, and so he wrote. He is glad that he did write now, for that 'Innocents Abroad,' written in that little back room on Indiana Avenue in Washington, has been the making of the fame and fortune of Mark Twain." Years later, J.H. Hoagland., Twain's landlord at his C Street boardinghouse, wrote to John Russell Young, "Sam Clements [*sic*] boarded in my house[.] [H]e wrote Inocents [*sic*] Abroad in the 2-story front room—he was there some 3 months."

Returning to Washington in early February 1868 from a trip to New York and Hartford, where he finalized the terms of his contract with the American

Publishing Company, Twain found twenty-eight letters awaiting his reply. His first answer was to Jacob H. Burrough, a friend from his youthful days in St. Louis. Twain wanted to share the recent turn of events in his life as an emerging man of letters with a confidant. The letter confirms Ramsdell's assertion that Twain "was writing for the money":

> *I have written 182 note-paper pages of newspaper matter at a dollar a page & 7 of magazine stuff at four dollars a page in the last two days. If I can write as much more in the next two days, I will be all right again. I just want to show them that when I make contracts, I am willing to fill them & then I will throw up all my correspondence except about $75 a week & sail in on my book—because I have made a tip-top, splendid contract with a great publishing house in Hartford for a 600-page volume illustrated—about the size of a Patent Office Report. My percentage is a fifth more than they have ever paid any man but Horace Greeley—I get what amounts to just about the same he was paid. But this is publisher's secret—keep it to yourself.*

Later that month, Twain wrote to his sister-in-law, confiding, "I have made a superb contract for a book & have prepared the first ten chapters of the sixty or eighty." Although by all accounts Twain's mind and actions were set on preparing his manuscript for *The Innocents Abroad*, his first book made a fleeting appearance in Washington City.

THE JUMPING FROG

When first published in the spring of 1867, *The Jumping Frog of Calaveras County* was "handsome," as Twain confessed to Bret Harte, but there were more pressing concerns. "It is full of damnable errors of grammar & deadly inconsistencies of spelling in the Frog sketch because I was away & did not read the proofs," Twain wrote. Before leaving Washington City to Hartford to negotiate his book contract, Twain had *The Jumping Frog* on his mind. Before retiring to bed at two o'clock in the morning on January 10, Twain composed a short letter to his inaugural publisher Charles Henry Webb. "Please send me 3 copies of…Frog," he wrote. "I never got but 6 of the lot you gave me an order for. I lost the order. Send them (the 3) through the mail." Twain wrote Webb on January 15, 1868, from "356 C bet. 4 ½ & 6th" letting him know that "the books came—am much obliged." Twain closed his letter, "I wished all the time that you were present."

Although there is not another extant letter between Twain and Webb for more than two years, Webb took Twain up on his appeal for company in Washington. On January 31, 1868 the *Evening Star* noted the conspicuousness of the two former San Francisco bohemians: "A Pair of 'Em!—[Charles] H. Webb, author of those clever burlesques 'Liffith Lank' and 'St. Twel'mo' was at the Capitol to-day, in company with a congenial spirit, 'Mark Twain.'" With no surviving written record between Twain and Webb, it is left to speculation what they did in Washington.

The next day, after the *Evening Star* noted Twain and Webb's presence together, Washington City's paper of record recognized that Webb, known by his *nom de plume*, John Paul, had attended the third weekly Friday evening reception of Speaker of the House Schuyler Colfax. Listing senators, congressmen, generals, judges, postmasters and department officials who had rubbed elbows, the short column closed by noting, "Frank Leslie, C. H. Webb (John Paul) and a host of others" had also been observed mingling. It is doubtful that Twain, who in a matter of weeks was listed in the *Star* and noted by Emily Edson Briggs as cutting quite a figure at one of Speaker Colfax's receptions, had stayed home.

In searching the *Morning Chronicle* for its review of a February Twain lecture in Georgetown, something unexpected was discovered: a line item ad for "The Jumping Frog. By Mark Twain. $1.50." at French & Richardson's bookstore. During Twain's time in Washington City as a capital correspondent, bookstores regularly advertised in the daily newspapers. The regulars were the Hudson Taylor Book Store, run by French & Richardson at 334 Pennsylvania Avenue; Blanchard & Mohun at the "corner [of] Pennsylvania avenue and Eleventh street"; Hunger's Great Antiquarian at "204 Penna. av. and 178 Penna. avenue"; W.M. Ballantyne at "519 Seventh street, Intelligencer Building"; Philip & Solomons' "Metropolitan Book Store, 332 Pennsylvania avenue"; and Shillington's Book Store at the corner of "Four-And-A-Half Street and Pennsylvania Avenue, Washington City." Although no advertisements appeared during the winter of 1867–68, James Guild had recently set up shop on the 100 block of Pennsylvania Avenue NW, a store that counted Twain as one of its famous patrons.

In reviewing the pages of the *Star* and the *Chronicle*, it is clear that French & Richardson's ran different ads in both papers at the same time. Twain's book is never included in the *Star* ads. Twain's *The Jumping Frog* was advertised five times on page three of the *Chronicle* as a "New Book" for sale at French & Richardson's

MARK TWAIN IN WASHINGTON, D.C.

NEW BOOKS. NEW BOOKS.

JUST RECEIVED AT

FRENCH & RICHARDSON'S

BOOKSELLERS AND STATIONERS,

334 PENNSYLVANIA AVENUE.

The Great Exhibition, with Continental sketches, &c. By H. P. Arnold. $2 25.

Cakes and Ale at Woodbine. By Barry Gray. $1 75.

Grandpa's House. By Helen C. Weeks. $1 50.

A French Country Family; translated from the French by the author of "John Halifax." $1 50.

The White Rose. By Melville. $1 50.

Meline: Two Thousand Miles on Horseback to Santa Fe and Back. $2.

Another new novel by Louisa Muhlback,

Old Fritz and the New Era. 1 vol.; cloth $2, paper $1 50.

The Jumping Frog. By Mark Twain. $1 50.

An ad for "The Jumping Frog. By Mark Twain. $1.50." at French & Richardson's, 334 Pennsylvania Avenue, ran in the *Daily Morning Chronicle* for five days, from February 18 to February 22, 1868. *DC Public Library, Washingtoniana Division.*

from February 18 through February 22. During this same time, French & Richardson's ran ads in the *Star* advertising discounted editions of Sir Walter Scott's Waverly Novels and the complete works of Charles Dickens. Whereas *The Jumping Frog* was not advertised in the *Star*, in the *Chronicle*, it was advertised as one of a dozen new books, including the "only official edition" of the *Trial of John H. Surratt* (a reoccurring newspaper story during Twain's sojourn in Washington).

In June 1867, Twain wrote the following in a letter to his family: "I don't believe [The Jumping Frog] will ever pay anything worth a cent. I published it simply to advertise myself & not with the hope of making anything out of it." From Buffalo the day after Christmas, 1870, Twain wrote a biographer, "I fully expected the 'Jumping Frog' to sell 50,000 copies & it only sold 4,000." With such limited distribution, how did *The Jumping Frog* appear in one of Washington City's most prominent bookstores?

Twain, along with Webb, could have simply walked in and pitched the book. When Webb came to Washington in late January, it is possible he brought extra copies of *The Jumping Frog* with him. Another possibility is that Twain received a supply of books from Routledge and Sons, which published *The Jumping Frog* in 1867. On January 20, 1868, Twain wrote his family that he had a "letter from Routledge, the London publisher, asking me to write for his magazine. Routledge says he is delighted with the Jumping Frog book & that it has a great sale in England. It has had a better sale in America than it deserved. It takes an awful edition to pay first cost, but it has done that—not many books do. I naturally suppose that *now* it will quit selling." French & Richardson's stock of *The Jumping Frog* appears to have been limited given that the book was advertised for than less than a week. During Twain's stay in Washington as a capital correspondent, French & Richardson's was one of the most prominent bookstores on the avenue.

"French & Richardson's Bookstore and adjacent structures were the last of dozens of federal brick buildings that once lined the Pennsylvania Avenue between the Capitol and the White House and were razed by the new Hoover FBI Building in 1963," writes James Goode in *Capitol Losses*.

French & Richardson's was a leading city bookstore on Pennsylvania Avenue in the nineteenth century. *Library of Congress.*

"The four-bay structure had its first floor converted to shop space at an early date. It was the home of the city's two outstanding bookstores of the nineteenth century—Taylor & Maury's Bookstore in the 1850s and French & Richardson's Bookstore in the 1860s."

According to journal entries and letters written by Walt Whitman while he was in Washington, he frequented city bookstores, including "Philip & Solomons' 332 Penn av. and French & Richardson 334." Both stores sold *Leaves of Grass*, Whitman's vaunted poetry collection. (Whitman and Twain were both in Washington during the winter of 1867–68, but there is no evidence of them having met.) Not only was French & Richardson's a destination for authors, but according to government reports at the time, it was also where government officials purchased books, literary journals, almanacs, stationery and other materials.

According to Paine, when Twain reached Washington City, his two concerns were to "make money" and "secure a government appointment for Orion." Paine contends that Twain "was moderately in debt" and "not immediately interested in the matter of book publication." By early March 1868, Orion had not received a position, but Twain was raising himself out of debt by working furiously as a journalist and beginning to visualize himself as an author. While in Washington, Twain got a jolt of adrenaline after seeing his book advertised in the city papers. This could only have added more fuel to the fire of Twain's ambitions, further expanding the horizon of his literary hopes.

CHAPTER 7
Mark Twain's Boardinghouses

*His room was always a sight—books, papers and newspaper clippings by the
bushel. He would not allow his room "tuched" and nothing to be disturbed. His
shoes of all kinds were in a row alongside of the wash board.*
—J.H. Hoagland to John Russell Young

When Twain settled in Washington for the winter of 1867–68, the city
was years away from being transformed into "New Washington."
The infrastructure improvements and building boom were yet to be fully
set in motion by the Grant administration and Board of Public Works, led
by Alexander Shepherd. But the municipality, uniquely built for the sole
purpose of national government and politics, had nevertheless changed in
the more than thirteen years since Twain had passed through as a teen-aged
rube. "The low-slung city was bigger, brisker, muddier and more crowded
with political parasites, buttonholers from railroad, timber, and mining
interests and other exemplars of the new America," writes a prominent
Twain biographer. Flocking to Washington, these people needed places
to stay. Since the beginning decades of the city, boardinghouses sheltered
congressmen, clerks, messengers, agents, waiters, journalists and all who took
up the ancillary vocations that supported Washington's legislative seasons.

In James Sterling Young's definitive work, *The Washington Community:
1800–1828*, the city's "boardinghouse fraternities," which "almost all
legislators joined when they came to Washington," are discussed in full.
These political frat houses were where members lived together, took their

meals together and enjoyed their leisure time in each other's company. These lodgings, known as messes, formed the "basic social units of the Capitol Hill community." Young writes, "Some legislators from the same state or region would travel together to the capital each fall and form themselves into a boardinghouse group upon arrival, perhaps recruiting others into their group to fill up the house." The "formalities and observances of society were not only disregarded but condemned as interferences with the liberty of person and freedom of speech and action." Boardinghouse affiliation became "a mark of identification among legislators." The communal experiences of early Washington's political boardinghouses, which Young so aptly chronicles, paralleled the camaraderie Twain enjoyed while living in literary boardinghouses during his stay in the national political mecca.

Throughout Twain's stay in Washington, he roomed in a collection of boardinghouses, a far cry from his subsequent returns to Washington in later years when he stayed in luxurious hotels such as the Arlington and the new Willard. His first room in Washington City was shared with his new boss, Senator Stewart, who remembered in his memoirs that it was "in a rather tumble-down building which at the time stood on the northwest corner of Fourteenth and F Streets, NW, opposite the old Ebbitt House, where many of my Congressional cronies had quarters. The house was a weather-beaten old place, a relic of early Washington." According to Stewart, the proprietress was Miss Virginia Wells, "an estimable lady about 70 years of age, prim, straight as a ramrod, and with smooth plastered white hair. She belonged to one of the first families of Virginia, which were quite numerous in Washington, and was very aristocratic; but having lost everything in the war, she had come to Washington and managed to make a precarious living as a lodging-house keeper." Stewart, who would later build a mansion off Dupont Circle known as "Stewart's Castle," had a spacious apartment on the second floor that faced both Fourteenth and F Streets in late 1867. Stewart divided the seventy-five-foot-long room "by a curtain drawn across it, making a little chamber at the rear, in which I slept." In the front was Stewart's sitting room, where he kept a desk, writing materials, books "and a sideboard upon which I kept at all times plenty of cigars and a supply of whiskey, for I occasionally smoked and took a drink of liquor."

More than forty years later, Stewart vividly remembered the day his famous secretary showed up: "I was seated at my window one morning when a very disreputable-looking person slouched into the room. He was arrayed in a seedy suit, which hung upon his lean frame in bunches with no style worth mentioning. A sheaf of scraggy black hair leaked out of a battered old slouch hat, like stuffing from an ancient Colonial sofa, and an evil-smelling cigar butt, very much frazzled, protruded from the corner of his mouth. He had a very sinister appearance. He was a man I had known around the Nevada mining camps several years before, and his name was Samuel L. Clemens." If Twain did not know where Stewart was lodging when he first reached Washington City, he could easily have found his address, along with near hundreds of other Congressmen and Senators, as it was printed in the newspaper announcing the legislators' arrivals.

Although Stewart was aware of Twain's disreputable reputation in Nevada, he allowed him to become "a member of my family" and room with him. The trouble soon began. "It was not long before Clemens took notice of Miss Virginia," Stewart recalled. "Her timid, aristocratic nature shrank from him, and I think she was half afraid of him. He did not overlook any opportunities to make her life miserable and was always playing jokes on her. He would lurch around the halls, pretending to be intoxicated, and would throw her into a fit about six times a day." The fits Twain put the old woman through were seemingly endless, lasting well into the night. Stewart further educed, "He would burn the light in his bedroom all night, and started her figuring up her expense account with a troubled, anxious face. Pretty soon he took to smoking cigars in bed."

Nighttime always haunted Twain's restless psyche, keeping him awake while others slept. In his seventies, he wrote, "[I]n my age, as in my youth, night brings me many a deep remorse. I realize that from the cradle up I have been like the rest of the race—never quite sane in the night." Writing in *Harper's Monthly Magazine* in 1891, Twain recalled a late summer evening spent in Washington in the 1870s when he was then staying at the Arlington Hotel. In his room, he "read and smoked until ten o'clock; then finding I was not yet sleepy, I thought I would take a breath of fresh air. So I went forth in the rain and tramped through one street after another in an aimless and enjoyable way." Although allegedly undirected and careless in his wandering, Twain "knew that Mr. O, a friend of mine, was in town, and I wished I might run across him; but I did not know where he was stopping." Around midnight, the streets were deserted, and to avoid his lonesomeness, Twain "stepped into a cigar shop far up the Avenue and remained there fifteen minutes, listening to some bummers discussing the national politics." Suddenly, a "spirit of prophecy" came over Twain, and he knew that if he walked outside, he would run into Mr. O, which he did.

Not everyone rustled so restlessly at night. After discovering Twain was up all night smoking cigars, Miss Virginia never slept, according to Stewart. The boardinghouse keeper lay awake every night "with her clothes handy on a chair, expecting the house to be burned down any minute and ready to skip out at the first alarm; and she became so pale, and thin, and wasted, and troubled that it would have melted a pirate's heart to see her." After a time, the old lady gave Stewart an ultimatum: "Senator, if you don't ask that friend of yours to leave, I shall have to give up my lodging-house, and God knows what will become of me then. He smokes cigars in bed all night and has ruined my best sheets, and I expect to be burned out any time. I've been on the alert now for three weeks, but I can't keep it up much longer. I need sleep."

Stewart beckoned his young secretary. "Clemens," Stewart said, "if you don't stop annoying this little lady, I'll give you a sound thrashing. I'll wait till that book's finished. I don't want to interfere with literature—I'll thrash you after it's finished." Stewart claimed that Twain responded by blowing smoke in his boss's face, before replying, "You are mighty unreasonable. Why do you want to interfere with my pleasures?" After issuing his warning, Stewart thought Twain would calm down. He did not, and Miss Virginia returned a week later, her eyes filled with tears. "Senator, that man will kill me," she said. "I can't stand it. If he doesn't go, I'll have to ask you to give up your rooms, and the Lord knows whether I'll be able to rent them again." Stewart was out of subtle warnings and issued Twain a threat: "If you don't cease annoying this little lady, I'll amend my former resolution and give you that thrashing here and now. Then I'll send you to the hospital, and pay your expenses, and bring you back, and you can finish your book upholstered in bandages." When and how Twain left the company of Stewart is unknown, but that he did (and consequently bounced from place to place) is clear from Twain's letters at the time, his later reminiscences and the memories of those he stayed with.

On February 21, 1868, Twain sent a letter to his family. With a return address of Stewart's boardinghouse at 224 F Street NW, Twain advised in the heading to "Keep your eye on the address." He opened the letter by writing, "Dear Folks—I was at 224 first— Stewart is there yet—I have moved five times since—shall move again, shortly. Shabby furniture & shabby food— that is Washn. I mean to keep moving." In an explanatory note for Twain's February 9 letter to Mary Mason Fairbanks, which was addressed from 76 Indiana Avenue, the editors of the Mark Twain Papers propose:

> *Clemens had presumably just moved to this address* [76 Indiana Avenue], *possibly from 356 C Street North, which he had given as the return address of his January 15 letter to* [Charles Henry] *Webb. It is also possible*

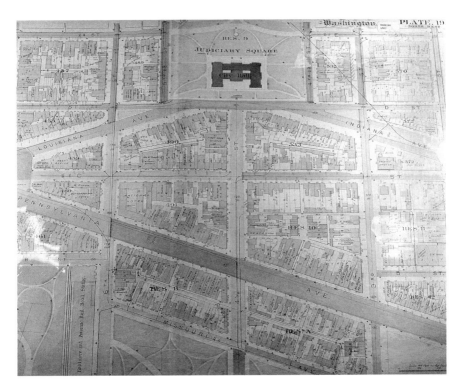

Mark Twain moved five times while in Washington City during the winter of 1867–68.
1887 Hopkins, Plate 19. *DC Public Library, Washingtoniana Division.*

that he left the C Street address when he went to New York and Hartford in January and then stayed again briefly with Senator Stewart at 224 F Street NW upon his return to Washington. In February, he would tell his family that he had moved five times since leaving Stewart's rooms, but only the C Street address and 76 Indiana Avenue—his current address—are known. Because he was moving frequently throughout this period, Clemens sometimes used 224 F Street for his return address, on the assumption that he could always collect his mail from Stewart, who still lived there.

It is also possible that Twain crashed an evening or two in the bureau office of the *New York Tribune* off Pennsylvania Avenue. In an 1883 newspaper article, Hiram J. Ramsdell recalled, "[Twain] made his headquarters at the Tribune Bureau and was not always welcome, for he was never goodnatured [*sic*] and was sometimes absolutely offensive, so much so that the correspondents did not always like to see him about." Not only did Twain haunt the Senate and

House press galleries, but it's possible Twain also frequented the city courts. If he rested at "356 C bet. 4½ & 6ᵗʰ," which he used as a return address once, and 76 Indiana Avenue, which he used twice, we can conclude that once Twain departed from under the roof of Senator Stewart, he spent his time in Washington City in and around this general area of Washington's Old City Hall, today the District of Columbia Court of Appeals.

Depending on when Twain began his search for new lodgings, it was either feast or famine in the boardinghouse market. On November 23, 1867, as legislators and their staffs were descending upon Washington for the start of the second session of the Fortieth Congress, the *Evening Star* advertised fourteen boardinghouses. "Transient and Permanent Boarders Can Obtain Desirable Rooms with Use of Bathroom (Hot and Cold Water), and First-Class Board, at the House Lately Occupied by the Nicaraguan Minister" read one ad, while another claimed "Strangers and Other Desirous of Obtaining First-Class Board and Handsomely Furnished Rooms, at Moderate Prices, Can Be Accommodated at the Newly-Opened House, No. 381 19ᵗʰ Street, Between G and H; One Square from the Cars; Five Minutes [*sic*] Walk from Departments." In late November, Twain could have been selective if he chose not to room with Stewart, but by February, his options were limited. A day after Twain wrote his family telling them he planned to move again, only four boardinghouses advertised in the *Evening Star*. Boarders advertised for rooms; a lone "Gentleman detained in Washington" was seeking "comfortable lodging and board, if the society is agreeable." However, Twain would not have been looking in the daily papers for a place to stay; his newly befriended Washington bohemians and literary men could easily provide referrals and a room.

"Around the Capital of a great nation, the artistic and literary spirits have always assembled, and this has been the case with Washington," George Alfred Townsend wrote in 1873 in *Washington, Outside and Inside*. Townsend, who moved to Washington and roomed with Twain in the winter of 1867-1868, delineated strict distinctions in describing the "four kinds of newspaper correspondence at the Capital City. First, the [Congressional] Globe; second, the Associated Press; third, the Special Telegraphers; fourth, the Special Correspondents." The last of these Townsend and Twain belonged to. "The special correspondents were amateur literary men, lookers-on in Washington, library readers, young office-holders with a destiny to throw ink, or people with a mission and a plethora of words."

As Twain remembered, he housed with a band of special correspondents and budding literary men. "I roomed in a house which also sheltered

BOARDING.

BOARDING. — Two pleasant FURNISHED ROOMS, in a private family, for rent, with BOARD and the comforts of a home; each suitable for gentleman and wife or two single gentlemen. Price $45 per month, (for two,) including fire and light. No. 517 I st., between 6th and 7th. fe22 3t*

GOOD BOARD, with comfortable ROOMS, in a healthy location and short distance from most of the Departments, can be had on reasonable terms at 218 K st., bet. 17th and 18th. fe 21-1m*

PLEASANT ROOMS, WITH FIRST-CLASS BOARD, at No. 441 5th street, between D and E, opposite City Hall. fe 19 3w

BOARD AND LODGING.—A GENTLEMAN detained in Washington desires comfortable Lodging and Board, if the society is agreeable. Address ORPHAN, P. O. fe 18-6t*

TABLE BOARD AT $20 PER MONTH—Served out at $25 per month—at 481 E street, between 3d and 4th, near City Hall. fe 14-eo6t*

BALLS, PARTIES, &c.

FIRST GRAND
MILITARY AND CIVIC BALL
TO BE GIVEN BY
POST No. 2, G. A. R.
At CARUSI HALL, corner 11th and C sts.,
TUESDAY, FEBRUARY 25TH.
Proceeds to be given to sick

"BOARDING," *Evening Star*, February 22, 1868. *DC Public Library, Washingtoniana Division.*

George Alfred Townsend, Ramsdell, George Adams, and Riley, of the San Francisco Alta." As Ramsdell remembered nearly two decades later, Twain was not the easiest person to room with at the "Indiana Avenue House." "I happened, with my wife and child, to be a boarder in that home," Ramsdell wrote. "For it was a regular Washington boarding house, with prices and accommodations slightly above the average." Among the boarders were "George Alfred Townsend—to me a most lovable fellow at that time—and his pretty wife; and then there was the handsome and manly Jerome B. Stillson, who was one of the most brilliant of war correspondents, the most intimate friend of President Johnson at that time doing magnificent work for the *New York World;* then there was Riley, of the Alta California, a character equal to any of Dickens' or Thackeray's." Tucked into "a little back room with a sheet-iron stove, a dirty, musty carpet of the cheapest description, a bed and two or three common chairs" was Mark Twain.

At the time, Ramsdell was a correspondent for the *New York Tribune,* which had published a handful of Twain's travel letters from his *Quaker City* trip. Fresh on Twain's return to the United States before lighting out for Washington, Ramsdell recalled, "[Twain] had been partly round the world and had seen a good deal. He looked at everything from the standing of a practical American and Western man and was 'green' enough to look at things through his own eyes and weigh things with his own common sense. He knocked the old reverence and awe all to thunder." Among the correspondents though, Ramsdell remembered, "Nobody knew him and nobody cared a rap for him. He was with Riley nearly all the time and was addicted to John Barleycorn."

As young correspondents, "[W]e all did our work in our rooms, and when one of us got tired we went to the room of one of the others. If the other fellow was working hard he snubbed the visitor, if he was idling he welcomed him." Twain did not follow this common etiquette. In his room, "the visitor was always welcomed, for by nature Twain is so lazy that he will not work if there is an excuse for loafing. He had a little back room that was a novelty, a museum, a hermit's cave, a den for a wild animal, and the wild animal was there." As a bachelor, Twain lived in abject squalor, Ramsdell recalled:

> [Twain's] *little drum stove was full of ashes, running over on the zinc sheet, which was covered all over; the bed seemed to be unmade for a week, the slops had not been carried out for a fortnight, the room was sour with tobacco-smoke, the floor, dirty enough to begin with, was littered with newspapers, from which Twain had cut his letters. Then there were hundreds of pieces of torn manuscripts which had been written and then rejected by the author. A dozen pipes were about the apartment—on the washstand, on the mantel, on the writing table, on the chairs—everywhere that room could be found. And there was tobacco and tobacco everywhere. One thing is that there were no flies. The smoke killed them, and I am now*

surprised that it did not kill me, too. Twain would not let a servant come into his room. He would strip down to his suspenders (his coat and vest, of course, being off), and walk back and forward in slippers in his little room and swear and smoke the whole day long. Of course, at times he would work, and when he did work, it was like a steam engine at full head.

One of Twain's closest companions during his stay in Washington City was John Henry Riley, the regular Washington correspondent for the *Daily Alta California* who moonlighted as a government clerk. During the first and second sessions of the Thirty-ninth Congress, Riley served as the clerk to the House Committee on the Pacific Railroad, for which he was paid a $200 bonus by a joint resolution. For the first session of the Forty-first Congress, Riley served as clerk to the House Committee on Mines and Mining while holding press credentials in the Reporter's Gallery of the Senate and the House. Riley surely educated Twain on how to work Washington for as much as it was worth, although from various accounts, including Twain's, Riley was always trying to stay one step ahead of imminent eviction.

"I think Riley is about the most entertaining company I ever saw," Twain wrote in the *Galaxy* in November 1870. "We lodged together in many places in Washington during the winter of '67–'68, moving comfortably from place to place and attracting attention by paying our board—a course which cannot fail to make a person conspicuous in Washington." During their adventures bebopping and flopping around Washington boardinghouses, Riley would enrapture Twain with tales "about his baking bread in San Francisco to gain a living, and setting up ten-pins, and practicing law, and opening oysters, and delivering lectures, and teaching French, and tending bar, and reporting for the newspapers, and keeping dancing school, and interpreting Chinese in the courts—which the latter was lucrative, and Riley was doing handsomely and laying up a little money when people began to find fault because his translations were too 'free,' a thing for which Riley considered he ought not to be held responsible, since he did not know a word of the Chinese tongue and only adopted interpreting as a means of gaining an honest livelihood." Apocryphal or not, it didn't matter; Twain remembered tales "Riley used to tell about publishing a newspaper up in what is Alaska now but was only an iceberg then, with a population composed of bears, walruses, Indians, and other animals; and how the iceberg got adrift at last and left all his paying subscribers behind." Twain and Riley were close enough friends that they joked about their own deaths, their landlord remembered years later. Twain "told Riley that he would write his Obituary some day—Riley said he would write his Son of Obituary."

One of the lasting memories Twain had of Riley was his "ready wit, a quickness and aptness at selecting and applying quotations, and a countenance that is as solemn and as blank as the back side of a tombstone when he is delivering a particularly exasperating joke." First reporting in the *Chicago Republican* on May 19, 1868, Twain recalled a distinct memory that he would repeat in print. "Once in Washington, during the winter, Riley, a fellow-correspondent, who stayed in the same house with me, rushed into my room—it was past midnight—and said, 'Great God, what can the matter be? What makes that awful smell?'" Twain replied, "Calm yourself, Mr. Riley. There is no occasion for alarm. You smell about as usual." Riley insisted that "there was no joke about this matter—the house was full of smoke—he had heard dreadful screams—he recognized the odor of burning human flesh." Twain and Riley soon confirmed the source. "A poor old negro woman, a servant in the next house," Twain wrote in the *Republican*, "had fallen on the stove and burned herself so badly that she soon died. It was a sad case, and at breakfast all spoke gloomily of the disaster and felt low-spirited. The landlady even cried, and that depressed us still more." Swept up in emotion, the landlady said, "Oh, to think of such a fate! She was so good and so kind and so faithful. She had worked hard and honestly in that family for twenty-eight long years, and now she is roasted to death." According to Twain, "in a grave voice and without even the shadow of a smile, Riley said: 'Well done, good and faithful servant!'" For Twain, a man who knew his Bible, he had to be familiar with Matthew 25:21, which reads, "His lord said unto him, Well done, thou good and faithful servant: thou hast been faithful over a few things. I will make thee ruler over many things: enter thou into the joy of thy lord." Nonetheless, given the solemnity of the death, Riley's words "sounded like a benediction, and the landlady never perceived the joke, but I never came so near choking in my life." In retelling the story in the *Galaxy* of November 1870, Twain slightly tweaked the details. He now remembered the landlady remarking, "I am but a poor woman, but even if I have to scrimp to do it, I will put up a tombstone over that lone sufferer's grave—and Mr. Riley, if you would have the goodness to think up a little epitaph to put on it which would sort of describe the awful way in which she met her....'" To which Riley responded, without ever smiling, "Put it 'Well done, good and faithful servant!'"

TWAIN'S NEIGHBORHOOD

Years after Mark Twain had moved on from the life of a Washington letter writer, his spirit had not been forgotten. In the process of compiling his memoirs in the 1890s, John Russell Young tracked down one of Twain's landlords, J.H. Hoagland, who showed Young where Twain boarded and some of the notable places in his neighborhood. Those sites could have included the extant former law offices of Daniel Webster at 503 D Street NW, a smattering of buildings at the corner of Fifth and Indiana Avenue NW (one houses a Subway sandwich shop today) that were built in the 1840s, and the Police Court Building at Sixth and D Street NW, which was razed in the mid-twentieth century.

The more immediate neighbor to Twain while he boarded in Hoagland's house was "Havener the Baker" who "lived next door," according to a previously unpublished letter Hoagland wrote to Young. It was Havener's servant who had fallen asleep and then "fell over on the hot stove and caught fire, and was roasted." According to the 1867 *Boyd's Directory of Washington City*, Thomas Havener and his son ran the bakery. To make clear which building housed Twain and which housed the bakery, Hoagland made a rudimentary sketch for Young.

Sketch of Mark Twain's C Street NW boardinghouse by J.H. Hoagland, his landlord. *Mark Twain Papers, UC Berkeley*.

Mark Twain in Washington, D.C.

In the late 1970s, legendary *Washington Post* newsman Chalmers R. Roberts described Mark Twain's old stomping grounds along the corners of 4½ Street: "The avenue between the Capitol and the White House nowadays is busier with new construction than at any time the Federal Triangle was under way half a century ago. At long last the small-town aura of the post–Civil War era is disappearing under the aegis of the Pennsylvania Avenue Development Corporation." More than a century before, Chalmers wrote, "In pre–Civil War decades, Elizabeth Peyton ran a 'select boardinghouse'" where today stands the Canadian Embassy. "Among its boarders were Chief Justice John Marshall, Henry Clay and John C. Calhoun. The building was remodeled, apparently around 1855, and beginning in 1869 became the Fritz Reuter's restaurant and rathskeller. Next door to Reuter's stood the city telegraph office until 1869; in an upper room was the first office of the original Associated Press." Due to the costs associated with telegraphing and the datelines of Twain's out-of-town correspondence, he made little use of the telegraph office. According to maps, records and Roberts, "Across the street, between 4th and 7th Streets, where the National Gallery stands today, was an elegant gambling establishment called the Palace of Fortune." In this vicinity of Pennsylvania Avenue, Twain's Washington neighborhood, were the city's leading bookstores and the office of the *Congressional Globe*, with the street cars and newspaper boys hawking the latest editions passed back and forth all day long.

CHAPTER 8

Twain Lectures Washington

I found out at 10 o'clock, last night, that I was to lecture to-morrow evening &
the next, & so you must be aware that I have been working like sin all night to
get a lecture written.
—Mark Twain

The production of Mark Twain's two public lectures in Washington in the winter of 1867–68 was, by his own account, "peculiar." After spending several days in New York and Hartford, Connecticut, where he saw Charles Dickens lecture, met his future wife, Olivia Langdon, for the first time and negotiated the particulars of his book contract with Elisha Bliss and the American Publishing Company, Twain arrived back in Washington, where he intended to catch up on his rest. "I arrived in the city at night and being tired did not care to leave the hotel for any purpose until morning," Twain recalled years later.

"When I opened the daily paper next morning at breakfast, what was my amazement to see an announcement in the advertising columns that I would deliver a lecture that evening at the old Lincoln Hall on the subject of the Sandwich Islands," Twain told a federal bureaucrat years later. "I had no such lecture on hand. Nobody had asked me to deliver such a lecture. Not a soul had spoken to me on the subject, nor had I spoken to anybody immediately or remotely hinting toward such a performance. To say that I was angry would imperfectly describe my mental condition. For once, language seemed too poor to enable me to do the subject justice. I longed to meet the miscreant or miscreants who had taken such liberties with my name."

The potential embarrassment of the situation dawned on the young man, who seemed to be turning a corner in his life toward respectability. This could set back what he had worked for. "Suppose I should make a public statement of the facts that the announcement of the lecture was without my authorization, knowledge or consent," Twain thought. "Half the community would not believe me. They would think there was some advertising dodge in some way connected with it." His appetite gone and breakfast left untouched on the table of his boardinghouse, Twain ventured into the city to see what damage had been done. "When I visited the hotel office, I found huge posters upon the walls making the same announcement as was contained in the newspaper advertising columns, and that the whole town had been billed in a thorough manner."

Without a repertoire of lectures on hand or in his head, Twain thought he was surely ruined. Before arriving in Washington in November 1867, his ally from out West, Frank Fuller, had notified him of outstanding invitations to lecture throughout the country. Twain declined. "I may be better known, then, after a winter spent in Washington," wrote Twain in response. Now he was obliged to deliver in order to save face, but first he sought out the source of the announcement.

"By a careful series of inquiries, I learned that an old personal friend of mine, whose libations sometimes led him into extravagancies and inconsistencies, had put up this job upon me, not through pique or malice, but in his exuberance at learning I was in the city, wanted to give a demonstration of his admiration for me," Twain reminisced without anger. "That explanation settled my fate. I saw I was in for it. I could not inform the public that the whole miserable business was the result of a drunken freak on the part of one of my personal friends. So I went to my room, denied myself to all visitors, and devoted that day to writing a lecture on the subject of the Sandwich Islands. "

Writing to his mother and sister on January 8, 1868, Twain confessed that although he had finished his lecture, "I don't think a very great deal of it. I call it 'Frozen Truth.' It is a little top-heavy, though, because there is more truth in the title than there is in the lecture." By happenstance, Charles Duncan, captain of the *Quaker City* excursion, was in Washington that night delivering a lecture at Metzerott Hall on Pennsylvania Avenue. Twain wrote to Emeline B. Beach, a fellow shipmate on the *Quaker City*, "When you see Capt. Duncan, I wish you would tell him how busy I am getting ready to tell the truth to-morrow night; I told him I would be present at his lecture this evening, but now I shall not be able to do it. Never mind—I WILL go & hear him to-night." If he had been free from composing his own lecture, Twain told Beach, he would "run about town & canvas for the Captain to-day. It wouldn't help his pocket any, but lecturers always like to have a crowded house."

The next night, Twain returned to the scene and made his Washington City debut at Metzerott Hall. "To say that the lecture and lecturer were a decided success is simply to record the verdict of a delighted audience," read a review in the *National Republican*. "The Frozen Truth" was a collection of "minor topics, humorous hits, and well-told anecdotes" recounting Twain's travels throughout "the Holy Land and various other points en route in Europe, Asia, and Africa." With physical descriptions of the ship and detailing the personal habits of the passengers, Twain "elicited uncontrollable bursts of laughter from the audience, while his reminiscences of the noble cities to-day and those of the past, visited by the voyagers, were given with all the genuine freshness of a traveler who has seen with observing eyes and a reflective mind all that he reproduces to his hearers."

In reviewing the lecture, the *Evening Star* devoted nearly two thirds of its front-page "News and Gossip" column to paraphrasing and quoting large portions of Twain's remarks and tersely describing his command and delivery. "Almost everybody who fancies he knows a good thing, in the humorous way, when he sees or hears it was on hand last night to assist at the debut of Mr. Clemens, otherwise known as 'Mark Twain,' as a lecturer," the article led off. Interjecting local flavor into his performance, Twain made the "mathematical comparison of the proportion of arable land to desert in Syria, to that of that of absolute lemon in the pies known as lemon pies, at his Washington hotel." The column further added, "His comparison of the public institutions, buildings and monuments of the U.S. to those of the Old World; his proud claim that no quarter of the Old World has such a monuments as the Washington Monument and that no officials there are more efficient and patriotic or collect their salaries more promptly than our members of Congress—these and a thousand other kindred touches and points served to give piquancy to the lecture." However, the *Star* remarked, "In the didactic portions, he was not so effective, his voice and style being not favorable to the expression of sentiment of pathos."

Overall, Twain was "not the kind of man the spectator 'expected to see,'" the *Star* concluded. "Of medium size, a cast-iron inflexibility of feature, grave face, eyes that lack expression from their natural hue and the light color of the brows, a drawling speech, and a general air of being half asleep," his "look for humor" was "very unpromising." Not yet a nationally known master of the stage, Twain's deliberative and distinctive style was already taking full form. "Many of the audience last night supposed that his slowness of speech and movement was stage mannerism, but that was a mistake. That imperturbable drawl is habitual to him, and he is probably the laziest walker that ever stepped. In his most fluent and vivacious moods, he has never been known to disgorge more than ten words per minute; and the saunter of Walt Whitman is a race-horse pace compared with his snail-like progress over the ground."

In summary, the *National Republican* offered, "Mark Twain possesses that rare but happy combination of talking as well as he writes; and if any of our readers may be laboring under a fit of the 'blues,' we recommend to them a speedy relief in the brief advice, 'Go and hear Mark Twain.' His next lecture is advertised for Saturday evening at the same place."

After making his Washington debut, Twain sat down to compose a letter to his family. "That infernal lecture is over, thank Heaven! It came near being a villainous failure," he began. Contradicting his memories years later, Twain wrote at the time, "It was not advertised at all. The manager was taken sick yesterday, & the man who was sent to tell me never got to me till after noon to-day. There was the dickens to pay. It was too late to do anything—too late to stop the lecture. I scared up a door-keeper,& was ready at the proper time, & by pure good luck a tolerably good house assembled & I was saved! I hardyly [*sic*] knew what I was going to talk about, but it went off in splendid style. I was to have preached again Saturday night, but I won't—I can't get along without a manager." Twain's leisurely stage manner belied all that was on his mind. He concluded his letter by writing, "I have got a thousand things to do & am not doing any of them. I feel perfectly savage. "

There would not be another lecture at Metzerott Hall, however. In a letter to the editor that was reprinted throughout Washington's daily papers on Saturday, January 11, 1868, Twain made a graceful exit. "I am sorry to see that the papers announce another lecture from me for this evening," he wrote. "I meant to be understood, last evening, as postponing the second lecture, but I suppose I was not. The gentleman who engaged me to lecture was taken very sick twenty-four hours before I was to address the public. (I had been reading my lecture to him, but upon my sacred honor, I did not think it would be so severe on him as that.) He is sick yet. I cannot lecture without an agent to attend to business. Please insert this for me and let it stand as a postponement of my lecture, until what time, the health of my unfortunate friend must determine. I will give him a chance though—I will not read the lecture to him anymore."

As the editors of the Mark Twain Papers point out, "Whatever problems were caused by this unidentified manager, Clemens also had a conflicting obligation, since he had agreed to respond to one of the toasts at the Washington Newspaper Correspondents' Club's annual banquet on the evening of Saturday, January 11. By the afternoon or evening of January 10, he had received still another reason to cancel the second performance," likely due to seeing his remarks reprinted in the *Evening Star*. Writing to the *Daily Alta California* with a dateline of January 11, Twain said:

> *I delivered a lecture here night before last—a new lecture. It went off well, but it was only a happy accident that it did, for there was nobody to attend to business. The newspapers are all exceedingly kind and complimentary, but one of them published a synopsis of the discourse. I was sorry for that, although it was so well meant, because one never feels comfortable, afterward, repeating a lecture that has been partly printed; and worse than that, people don't care about going to hear what they can buy in a newspaper for less money. I beg that the Coast papers will not print any synopsis of my sermons they may find floating around.*

FORREST HALL AND THE AGED WOMAN'S HOME OF GEORGETOWN

Walking down lower Wisconsin Avenue NW following a visit to the Peabody Room of the Georgetown Branch of the DC Public Library, I passed Ms. Geraldine Sapp, who, seeing me approach, offered an invitation. "Are you saved, young man? You look like you're bound to do the Lord's work. Have you ever been to Bible Way Church on New Jersey Avenue? You're always welcome; tell them Mama Sapp sent you."

Ms. Sapp, originally from Tampa, Florida, is one of a dozen residents at the Aged Woman's Home of Georgetown at 1255 Wisconsin Avenue, an organization founded in 1868 that has a little-known connection to Mark Twain. Perched above the street, located in a home built before the founding of the country and once visited by George Washington, the Aged Woman's Home is a quiet sanctuary in the middle of the city, seemingly unnoticed by the thousands of tourists, shoppers, diplomats, teenagers, college students, lawyers, politicians, journalists, socialites, artisans and others who pass

Geraldine Sapp brings her ministry to 1255 Wisconsin Avenue NW outside of the Aged Woman's Home of Georgetown. *Photo by author.*

through Georgetown every day. An occupancy permit from the city issued in the 1950s hangs on a rear wall alongside prints of the Corcoran Museum recognizing William Corcoran, whose initial donation of $15,000 founded the Ladies Union Benevolent Society following the Civil War. By the front door is an oversized pictorial Bible from the late 1840s.

Forrest Hall, circa 1921, Commercial Photo Company, 1403 H Street, NW. Today it is the Gap. *Collection of Peabody Room, DC Public Library.*

Across the street from the Woman's Home is a Gap clothing store at 1258 Wisconsin Avenue. More than 150 years ago, the three-story Greek Revival building was Forrest Hall, an assembly hall where Mark Twain gave a beneficiary lecture. Named for its owner, wealthy Georgetown resident Bladen Forrest, the building opened in 1851. Forrest Hall's meeting rooms hosted groups like the Masons and the Woman's Christian Temperance Union, who discussed issues such as retroceding Georgetown back to Maryland. During the Civil War, the building became Forrest Hall Military Prison, an improvised jail for deserters where three people died, according to government records. This was the site of the last public lecture Twain delivered while in Washington.

On Saturday, February 22, 1868, the *Georgetown Courier* ran a notice that "Mark Twain, the genial, witty and humorous Californian" would be "volunteering his services" for "the benefit of the Ladies' Union Benevolent Society" later that evening. According to the *Daily Morning Chronicle*, an "appreciative audience, including many of the most prominent persons of Georgetown," packed Forrest Hall that night:

> [Twain] *selected as his topic "The Sandwich Islands" and for an hour or more kept the audience in almost continuous roars of laughter. Upon stepping forward to the desk in his usual cautious and deliberate manner, he was received with applause. He apologized for his appearance without an introduction by stating that the young man who had promised to present him to the audience has been disabled. He fell down and broke his heart or neck. Mark didn't know which, not being particularly interested in the young man. The chief reason for his intrusion upon their attention was a request, made by several ladies, that he should deliver a lecture for the poor. He always had a grudge against the poor and therefore embraced the opportunity to inflict a lecture on them.*

CHAPTER 9

Capital Misadventures

I sent a resignation of my Congressional honors to the Speaker of the
House of Representatives.
—Mark Twain

Throughout Mark Twain's sojourn in Washington City, he had misadventures—real and imagined—in and around Congress. According to the written trail he left behind, Twain resigned as private secretary in a flurry, was impeached after attempting to address the floor of the House and was fired as the doorkeeper of the Senate. Through the personal notebook he kept, the stories he wrote while in the city as a capital correspondent and accounts of his attending social functions, a flamboyant portrait of a young man pushing the boundaries of proper etiquette and decorum emerges. Without needing much provocation, Twain filled the role of a literary hit man while in the capital. As John Russell Young wrote in his unpublished memoirs, "[Twain] wrote brilliant political letters from Washington. By request, he satirized Secretary Seward's plan for buying St. Thomas Island for a Naval Station." The purchase of Alaska was still a current affair and "had been ridiculed as a waste of more than seven millions [*sic*] for icebergs and Polar bears, and Mark Twain called attention to the earthquake features of the Island of St. Thomas. His uncle, he said, who owned a brick yard there, got up one morning and found it in the sky." Whatever popularity there was for "the proposed St. Thomas purchase," Twain helped kill with his article

"Information Wanted," published in the *New York Tribune* on December 18, 1867. He was only getting started.

"One wishes these notes might continue," Albert Bigelow Paine concluded when publishing, for the first time in 1935, the short "thumb-nail sketches" Twain wrote of Representatives of the House for the Fortieth Congress. In all, Twain jotted notes about eighteen congressmen from all parts of the country, including Wisconsin, New York, Illinois, Ohio, Pennsylvania, Maryland and Tennessee. The last congressman he documented, however briefly, was William Robinson, one of the earliest Washington letter writers. It was on his shoulders that Twain stood as a capital correspondent.

Twain's shortest notation was for Samuel Shellabarger of Ohio, whom Twain described simply as "able." James Garfield, also of Ohio and the future president of the United States, was "young, able, and scholarly—was chief of Rosecrans—preacher." William B. Allison of Iowa wore a "sack-coat" and "light-blue pants" which made him look "like a village law student," according to Twain. Allison "plays for handsome looks—30—hands in pockets—excessively ordinary-looking man—large flat foot—light handsome brown hair—youngest-looking member—essentially ornamental—stands around where woman can see him." Representative Francis Thomas of Maryland, a former governor, "belongs to another age—Whig—old style—hermit in every way—woman-hater—lives up in the mountains along in N.W. Maryland—one of the oldest Reps—is a radical."

The appearance and mannerisms of Benjamin Butler, a major general in the Union army now representing Massachusetts, particularly struck Twain, who described him thusly: "[The] forward part of his bald skull looks raised like a water-blister—its boundaries at the sides and at its base in front is marked by deep creases—fat face—small dark moustache—considerable hair behind and on the side—one reliable eye. Is short and pursy—fond of standing up with hands in pants pockets and looking around to each speaker with the air of a man who has half a mind to crush them and yet is rather too indifferent. Butler is dismally and drearily homely, and when he smiles it is like the breaking of a hard winter." In the coming months, Butler would play a leading role in the House's impeachment of President Andrew Johnson.

With the political air thick in Washington, Twain described radical Republican Thaddeus Stevens of Pennsylvania as the "ablest man" and Charles Eldredge from Wisconsin as a "leading and malignant copperhead." However serious the back and forth between the president and Congress, Twain made note of a future object of his biting humor: Representative John Logan of Illinois, who would later become a senator and presidential hopeful. Logan had "black eyebrows long black implacable straight hair, without a merciful curve in it—big black moustache—pleasant look in eye." Twain took issue not with his appearance or politics but his humor. Logan, Twain wrote, "often & even makes bad jokes sometimes, but tigers play in a ponderous sort of way. Splendid war record—15th Army Corps and Army of Tenn.—1 of Sherman's generals—better suited to war than making jokes."

While working for a handful of newspapers, Twain also attempted to maintain his secretaryship. In the May 1868 issue of the *Galaxy*, he laid bare the facts, as he saw them, of what led to his resignation as secretary for Nevada senator James W. Nye. According to Twain, "I held the berth

Before coming to Washington, Twain knew Nevada senator James W. Nye from his coverage of the territorial legislature. *Library of Congress.*

two months in security and in great cheerfulness of spirit, but my bread began to return from over the waters then—that is to say, my works came back and revealed themselves." One early morning, Senator Nye sent for Twain as he was finishing "inserting some conundrums clandestinely into his last great speech upon finance." Twain noticed something was out of order. The senator's "cravat was untied, his hair was in a state of disorder, and his countenance bore about it the signs of a suppressed storm. He held a package of letters in his tense grasp, and I knew that the dreaded Pacific mail was in."

The senator told Twain, "I thought you were worthy of confidence." Twain replied that he was, although clutched in Nye's hand was evidence to the contrary. "I gave you a letter from certain of my constituents in the State of Nevada, asking the establishment of a post office at Baldwin's Ranch, and told you to answer it as ingeniously as you could with arguments which should persuade them that there was no real necessity for an office at that place," Nye said. Twain responded that he had complied, to which Nye confirmed, "Yes, you did. I will read your answer, for your own humiliation":

WASHINGTON, NOV. 24, 1867
Messrs. Smith, Jones, and Others

GENTLEMEN: What the mischief do you suppose you want with a post office at Baldwin's Ranch? It would not do you any good. If any letters came there, you couldn't read them, you know; and besides, such letters as ought to pass through, with money in them, for other localities, would not be likely to get through, you must perceive at once; and that would make trouble for us all. No, don't bother about a post office in your camp. I have your best interests at heart and feel that it would only be an ornamental folly. What you want is a nice jail, you know—a nice, substantial jail and a free school. These will be a lasting benefit to you. These will make you really contented and happy. I will move in the matter at once.

Very truly, etc.,
MARK TWAIN,
For James W. Nye, U.S. Senator

Nye was beside himself: "That is the way you answered that letter. Those people say they will hang me if I ever enter that district again—and I am perfectly satisfied they will, too." Twain was bemused: "Well, sir, I did not know I was doing any harm. I only wanted to convince them." Nye agreed with "no manner of doubt" that Twain had done what he asked but had gone about it in the wrong way. The senator had another example: "I gave you a petition from certain gentlemen of Nevada, praying that I would get a bill through Congress incorporating the Methodist Episcopal Church of the State of Nevada. I told you to say, in reply, that the creation of such a law came more properly within the province of the State Legislature; and to endeavor to show them that, in the present feebleness of the religious element in that new commonwealth, the expediency of incorporating the church was questionable. What did you write?"

Once again, Twain had complied without thinking of the retribution he might incur:

WASHINGTON, Nov. 24, 1867
Rev. John Halifax and Others

GENTLEMEN: You will have to go to the State Legislature about that little speculation of yours—Congress don't know anything about religion. But don't you hurry to go there either, because this thing you propose to do out in that new country isn't expedient—in fact, it is simply ridiculous. Your religious people there are too feeble, in intellect, in morality, in piety— in everything, pretty much. You had better drop this—you can't make it work. You can't issue stock on an incorporation like that—if you could, it would only keep you in trouble all the time. The other denominations would abuse it, and "bear" it, and "sell it short," and break it down. They would do with it just as they would with one of your silver mines out there—they would try to make all the world believe it was "wild cat." You ought not to do anything that is calculated to bring a sacred thing into disrepute. You ought to be ashamed of yourselves—that is what I think about it. You close your petition with the words: "And we will ever pray." I think you had better—you need to do it.

Very truly, etc.,
MARK TWAIN,
For James W. Nye, U.S. Senator

Due in part to Twain's letter, Nye was finished with "the religious element among my constituents." Regrettably, Twain had responded to two other letters in similar form and fashion, prompting Nye to tell him to "leave the house! Leave it forever and forever, too!" Twain got the message. "I regarded that as a sort of covert intimation that my services could be dispensed with, and so I resigned," he recalled. "I never will be a private secretary to a senator again. You can't please that kind of people."

However long or short Twain's tenure as a private secretary truly was, his position as doorkeeper of the Senate was equally momentary. Written with a dateline of December 15, 1867, his Washington letter describing his latest parody of official life was published in the *New York Citizen* on December 21. After resigning the office of page of the House of Representatives, Twain "rejoined Mr. Johnson's Administration as Doorkeeper of the Senate." Twain did not wait to make the most of his new position: "On the first morning of my occupation of my new post, I locked all the entrances to the Senate Chamber but one and took my station there. Presently, a gentleman approached and tried to pass in. I stopped him." Senator Benjamin Franklin Wade of Ohio, who at that time was the president of the Senate, identified himself before this novel doorkeeper. "Wade...Wade. I don't remember hearing of you before. Is that your regular name, or is it a nom de plume?" Twain asked incredulously, revealing his political illiteracy. Wade then produced his credentials. "Considering that he was the ringmaster of the circus, I let him in free," Twain wrote. "But I had trouble with the others. Some of them had no credentials and had to stay out. I taxed the balance fifty cents admission, and as soon as they got a quorum, they passed a resolution of instruction to the Sergeant-at-Arms, and I was arrested and compelled to disgorge. This high-handed usurpation of power came near making another split between myself and the Government, but I submitted and resolved to bide my time."

During afternoon debates, Twain thought it appropriate to participate. Senator Wade rebuked the petty bureaucrat: "Silence! The Doorkeeper will resume his station by the door." Twain was resolute: "From this time forward, for three days, I could never get the floor. I was snubbed every time I attempted to speak; whenever a viva voce vote was taken, my voice did not affect the result; when there was a division, I was not counted, either when I stood up or sat down; when there was a call of the house, my name was studiously omitted by the Secretary and his minions." Twain swore no party allegiance: "I frequently voted on both sides of the same question, purposely to catch the Secretary, and I succeeded. During all this time, the galleries were filled with people from all parts of the country who were anxious to hear me speak. No matter—their feelings were not respected—the venomous persecution went on." On the fourth day, Twain once again interrupted Senate debate and was restrained by the sergeant at arms.

Similar to his secretaryship, Twain's position as doorkeeper would come to an unexpected and unglamorous end. On the fifth day, the Judiciary Committee presented two reports. A majority of five members "brought in a wild document, which they styled 'Articles of Impeachment against the Doorkeeper of the United States Senate,'" Twain alleged. "The minority, of four members, reported against the impeachment." The Articles of Impeachment charged Twain with violating the Constitution of the United States. "The infamy of the Senate is complete," Twain concluded. "Their work is done, and I stand before my country today a Doorkeeper on Sufferance! But firm as a rock, I stand at my post and await the verdict."

Soon after his removal as Senate doorkeeper, Twain managed to secure appointment as "clerk of the Senate Committee on Conchology," apparently established for the study of a form of seashells. Written with a dateline of December 2, 1867, and published in the *New York Tribune* on December 27, Twain's sketch, "The Facts Concerning My Resignation," was included in his *1875 Sketches New and Old* and subsequent volumes of his writings during his life. As Twain wrote, "If I were to detail all the outrages that were heaped upon me during the six days that I was connected with the government in an official capacity, the narrative would fill a volume."

Apparently, Twain let his minor position get to his head and thought it within bounds to seek out Secretary of the Navy Gideon Welles and insist that Admiral David Farragut come home to the United States from abroad. When Welles asked Twain who he was, Twain responded that he was "a member of that same government, clerk of the Senate Committee on Conchology." Welles promptly ordered Twain to "leave the premises and give my attention strictly to my own business in future. My first impulse was to get him removed. However, that would harm others besides himself and do me no real good, and so I let him stay."

Twain next went to see Edwin Stanton, secretary of war, "who was not inclined to see me at all until he learned that I was connected with the government." Twain was admitted, he claimed. While the alleged clerk took no issue with Stanton's "defending the parole stipulations of General Lee and his comrades in arms," Twain "could not approve of his method of fighting the Indians on the Plains." After Twain had finished expressing his discontent, Stanton asked Twain if he was a member of the Cabinet. Twain replied that he was: "[Stanton] inquired what position I held, and I said I was clerk of the Senate Committee on Conchology. I was then ordered under arrest for contempt of court and restrained of my liberty for the best part of the day." Twain was momentarily "resolved to be silent thenceforward and let the Government get along the best way it could."

However, duty called, Twain said, and he obeyed by calling on the secretary of the treasury. At issue was Twain's displeasure with the "extravagant length of his report," which was "expensive, unnecessary, and awkwardly constructed; there were no descriptive passages in it, no poetry, no sentiment—no heroes, no plot, no pictures—not even wood-cuts. Nobody would read it—that was a clear case. I urged him not to ruin his reputation by getting out a thing like that. If he ever hoped to succeed in literature, he must throw more variety into his writings. He must beware of dry detail. I said that the main popularity of the almanac was derived from its poetry and conundrums and that a few conundrums distributed around through his Treasury report would help the sale of it more than all the internal revenue he could put into it." The secretary did not appreciate Twain's "meddling with his business" and threatened to throw him out of the window. Upset that he was not shown the proper deference, Twain concluded the treasury secretary, fresh off his report, "was just like a new author. They always think they know more than anybody else when they are getting out their first book. Nobody can tell them anything."

Distressed at the treatment he had thus received, Twain felt there was a larger conspiracy at work "from the very beginning to drive me from the Administration." During his transitory clerkship, he claimed to have crashed one Cabinet meeting at the White House. When the president asked his credentials, Twain handed him a card that read, "The HON. MARK TWAIN, Clerk of the Senate Committee on Conchology." Johnson looked Twain "from head to foot, as if he had never heard of me before." The secretaries of treasury, war and navy all spoke up and against "this youth." Twain persisted in his desire to attend the meeting. Secretary of State Seward stepped in. "Young man, you are laboring under a mistake," Seward said. "The clerks of the Congressional committees are not members of the Cabinet. Neither are the doorkeepers of the Capitol, strange as it may seem. Therefore, much as we could desire your more than human wisdom in our deliberations, we cannot lawfully avail ourselves of it. The counsels of the nation must proceed without you; if disaster follows, as follow full well it may, be it balm to your sorrowing spirit that by deed and voice you did what in you lay to avert it. You have my blessing. Farewell." This dismissal was satisfactory, and Twain left peacefully.

Upon returning to his "den in the Capitol" and placing his "feet on the table like a representative," Twain was approached by a senator on the nonexistent Conchological Committee who was in a fury and asked where he had been all day. For the past three days, there had been work to do, the Senator said, "of copying a report on bomb-shells, egg-shells, clamshells, and I don't know what all connected with conchology." In protest, Twain responded, "Sir, do you suppose that I am going to work for six dollars a day? If that is the idea, let me recommend the Senate Committee on Conchology to hire somebody else. I am the slave of no faction! Take back your degrading commission. Give me liberty, or give me death!" Twain was let go. "Snubbed by the department, snubbed by the Cabinet, snubbed at last by the chairman of a committee I was endeavoring to adorn, I yielded to persecution, cast far from me the perils and seductions of my great office, and forsook my bleeding country in the hour of her peril." But Twain would not go quietly and submitted an expense report charging $36 for his six days as clerk, $150 for his consultation with the three Cabinet secretaries and $2,800 for his travels with the justification that "[t]erritorial delegates charge mileage both ways, although they never go back when they get here once." He was approved for his daily pay and denied the other requests.

For the moment, Twain was done with official life: "Let those clerks who are willing to be imposed on remain. I know numbers of them in the departments who are never informed when there is to be a Cabinet meeting, whose advice is never asked about war, or finance, or commerce, by the heads of the nation, any more than if they were not connected with the government, and who actually stay in their offices day after day and work!" His next caricature of Washington life would involve him not in a mere routine appointment but directly representing the American people. Appearing in the *New York Tribune* on February 13, 1868, with a dateline of February 9, "The Facts Concerning the Recent Important Resignation" is the crowning achievement of Twain's brush with formal Washington. "I have resigned once more. The circumstances were these," Twain begins. "The Hon. Mr. Axtell, member of the House of Representatives from California, requested me to act in his stead in Congress for a few days, during which he was obliged to be absent. The President of the United States, and also the Pacific delegation of Senators, urged me to comply with that request, believing, as they were kind enough to say, that I could settle this Reconstruction business if I would throw the weight of my wisdom into it. Thus importuned, I consented to overlook former ill-treatment and connect myself with the Government once more in an official capacity." According to Twain, on February 5, he "became a member, ad interim, of the House of Representatives" and "entered at once upon the duties of the position."

The story begins with Congressman John Logan protesting to the Speaker "against any gentlemen publishing in *The Globe* remarks purporting to have been made in this House in answer to another gentlemen but never actually delivered." Logan's colleague from Illinois, Samuel Marshall, rose in self-defense, stating, "I do not admit the right of my colleague, from any position that he occupies here or before the country, to become my censor in regard to anything here or elsewhere." In response, Logan took offense at Marshall's "insinuations that Logan was 'an illiterate man.'" Marshall quickly retorted, "I do not desire to carry this any further. My colleague is mistaken; I made no reference to his education. I do not know whether he is educated or not."

Logan came back: "If, as he says, it is the custom of the House to inject in *The Globe* speeches never made in this House, that custom ought to be abolished this very day, for it is infamous that the people should be taxed dollar after dollar to pay for speeches that are written by lawyers in this city, handed to a member, and published in *The Globe*. Sir, there is no parallel for this except when two gentlemen from Ohio read the same speech, one a few days after the other, probably written for both by the same person."

Ready to end the back and forth, Marshall offered, "I have made the statement that the speech published is the speech delivered by me on that occasion with the additions which I have explained, and which I referred to at the time, before taking my seat, and there are several gentlemen around me who remember the fact. If my colleague expects to make any reputation by the display he has made here this morning, he is entirely welcome to all he can gain thereby." Marshall concluded by uttering a word unprintable, which the Speaker rejected as unparliamentary.

"I take it back," Marshall said. "I withdraw the ****," which elicited laughter. Marshall continued, "I would commend to my friend hereafter when he is disturbed by feelings such as have disturbed him this morning to procure a bottle of Mr. Winslow's Soothing Sirup [*sic*], or perhaps Jayne's Carminative Balsam would be better to relieve him from such pains as have been agitating him this morning. If that does not produce the desired effect, if he will get a bottle of good, strong vermifuge, he will most unquestionably be relieved from the pains which have been weighing him down."

Logan was short in his reply: "I will say to the gentleman and to this House that I am too much a gentleman to reply to any indecent language, such as has been used by the gentlemen who claims to be a gentlemen; whether he is or not has never been determined by a jury."

In an effort to put the crude behavior behind them for the day, the Speaker recognized a fictitious congressman, "Mr. Rawhide." Wasting no time, Mr. Rawhide took the floor:

I have several times sought this opportunity to place myself on record upon this great question of Reconstruction, but I have always been forestalled by one driveling idiot or another upon this floor. I am happy to know that the time has at last arrived when I may freely lift my feeble voice on behalf of my suffering country. I have listened to the sneaking hypocrisy of the gentleman (Mr. Lipservice) from one state upon this grand subject. I have listened to the coarse brutality of the gentleman (Mr. Muscle) from another, upon the Reconstruction laws. I have listened to the monstrous lies of the gentleman (Mr. Ananias) from another, concerning the matter of constitutionality. I have listened to the nauseating tirades of a dozen other gentlemen, Sir, upon the all-absorbing topic; but Sir, none of these have speeches have convinced me—none of them have constructed me—they have failed to extinguish the sacred fountain of my patriotism or befoul its pure fires with wrathful deluges they have exhaled from the festering Augean stables of their degraded souls! Lies will not do, Sir! Brutality cannot convince, Sir! Sneaking villainy, base hypocrisy, balderdash, billingsgate, fall from the lips of Congressmen unheeded by me, when I know that their object is to blind me to the best interests of my country by these dazzling flights of deceptive eloquence.

The Speaker interrupted this soliloquy, requesting "him to yield it a moment to the member ad interim from California, in compliance with an honored custom of the House, which gives a new member an opportunity himself, if he desires to do so." Mr. Rawhide complied. "Certainly, certainly. I yield to the cur." Now was his moment. The Honorable, ad interim, Mr. Twain stepped forward.

"Mr. Speaker, when the proud bird of freedom spreads his broad pinions…" was all Twain could utter before being interrupted by the fabricated Mr. Ananias, who said, "I call this innocent ass to order. The proud bird of freedom is not before the House." Twain responded, "I scorn the interruptions of lying miscreants. Sir, when the proud bird of freedom spreads his broad pinions…" before Logan interjected. Twain redoubled his effort: "I scorn also the feeble wit of savages from the wilds of Illinois. Sir, when the proud bird of freedom spreads…" Now Zachariah Chandler from Michigan exclaimed, "Why, let her spread, fool!" "Silence!" Twain retorted. "You pitiful gutter-snipe! Mr. Speaker, I perceive here a disposition on the part of gentlemen to deny to me that courtesy which is due to gentlemen in my position. Sir, this is the first time I have ever had the privilege of appearing before this illustrious company of blackguards, and I feel a natural delicacy about intruding my views so early upon their attention. My duty to my constituents, however, imperatively demands that I should place myself upon record at once. I therefore beg leave to repeat, Sir, that when the proud bird of freedom…" Mr. Marshall returned to his stock joke, saying, "Well, this drawling parrot is certainly troubled with ****!"

Twain sought help: "Mr. Speaker, manifestly I cannot proceed if I am to be constantly interrupted by this Hoosier vagrant and the slang-dispensing varlets who have preceded him in the same business. I will now take my seat, Sir, preserving to myself the floor for this morning hour to-morrow, at which time I shall be ready with a speech in their own atrocious dialects which will scorch these puny sand-pipers as they were never scorched before." And that was the end of his career as a congressman.

"I was not permitted to keep my word," Twain confessed. "At 7 o'clock that evening, I was summoned to appear before the honorable corporation known as the Newspaper Correspondents' Club. I trembled then, for I could guess what was coming. I found a full board present." The president admonished him with a strong reprimand and fine:

Mr. Twain, it grieves me to state that you have been found guilty of conduct unbecoming a respectable member of the community, and especially unbecoming a member of this Club. You have so far forgotten yourself as to descend to the rank of a common Congressman. Pause and reflect upon the style of men these people are. They are sent here by a confiding people to carry out in an honorable and dignified manner the behests of a great nation. In authority they rank, as a body, above the President himself. They hold that place which, in other hands, is sacred to royalty alone. How do they show their appreciation of their great office? By uttering offensive personalities—slang—inferior wit—unnecessary and procrastinating speeches upon unimportant matters—and sometimes, alas! Language that tinges the cheeks of ladies in the galleries with a blush. These things are not done by all of these gentlemen; but are not they that permit them, unrebuked, accessories to the wrong, and therefore guilty, also? Mr. Twain, we cannot listen to explanations. You have outraged our dearest sensibilities and must receive our sentence in silence. You are suspended from all voice in the Club for the space of thirty days; you are fined the sum of five hundred dollars; you are commanded to appear no more in Congress.

Twain was left with no choice: "I sent a resignation of my Congressional honors to the Speaker of the House of Representatives."

CHAPTER 10

The Gay and Busy Season

Mark Twain, the delicate humorist, was present; quite a lion, as he deserves to be.
—Emily Edson Briggs

A bsent Washingtonians are getting back in time for the gay and busy season just now beginning," wrote the *Evening Star* less than a week before Mark Twain arrived on the Washington scene. A couple days later, the same paper noted, "'Mark Twain,' of humorous renown, is in Washington for the Winter and can be counted upon for something lively for the columns of the *New York Tribune* and *California Alta.*" The *National Republican* announced Twain was in town "taking a look at the American (political) Mecca." As it turned out, his time in the city would not be entirely devoted to analyzing the political system within the strict walls of Congress and committee rooms; while in Washington, Twain did not shy from the social life. During his short stay in Washington, he "found himself all at once in the midst of receptions, dinners, and speech-making; all very exciting, for a time at least, but not profitable, not conducive to work." If Twain was going to get a full portraiture of Washington, he had to hit the cosmopolitan town.

"When all is said, though, there is not much else in Washington but official life," wrote an early twentieth-century capital correspondent. "The gradations of official life create corresponding degrees in the social life of the city. There are sets without end here. There is the Cabinet set, the diplomatic set, the Senatorial set, the Congressional set, the army and navy set, the department clerk set." Additionally, a "special set of the retired rich, and there is another for the aristocratic persons who may or may not have visible means of support" played the scene. "To climb from one set to another is the dream of the Washingtonian," J. Fredrick Essary explained. "All of them do not climb, but all of them try to; and there is no psychological difference between those who do climb and those who fail. Some of them may not graduate from the euchre parties of the department clerk set, yet all of them abide in the hope of some day receiving an invitation to a Congressional ball, or a Senatorial dinner, or even to a Secretary's at-home."

In one of his dispatches for the *Chicago Republican*, Twain gave a brief sketch of how people were perpetually trying to advance themselves in Washington. One day, Twain was absently standing by himself while "reading a vast law book" in the chamber of the Senate Judiciary Committee "when a youth to fortune and to fame unknown flourished in the most frisky way and came to a halt before me." After stroking his undergrown moustache, the young man bellowed "Hello!" Twain replied with an equal response, which surprised the youth and provoked him to ask Twain, "Do you belong here?" Twain responded by remarking on the weather, which caused the youth to prance around the room before asking, "Are you the clerk on the Judiciary Committee?"

Twain responded indirectly, asking the youth, "In view of the circumstance that on so short an acquaintance you betray so much solicitude concerning my business, I will venture to inquire again what you may happen to want with the clerk of the Judiciary Committee." After the youth said it was none of his business, Twain repeated himself to the inquisitive chap, causing him to scratch his head. "Well, I'll be damned," the lad said. "I presume so," Twain responded. "I hope so. Still, being a stranger, you cannot expect me to take more than a passing interest in your future plans." Disgruntled, the young "fire brand" sauntered off on his own to make an inquiry of the Michigan senators he sought.

Twain later learned that that the strange "young party" with the "imaginary moustache" was an "importation from Kalamazoo" who "wished to ship as a sub-clerk to the Judiciary Committee." Twain thought the fellow was a "little fresh" and in need of more seasoning at "the Kalamazoological Gardens until he got his growth, perhaps." However, Twain saw something in the youth he admired. "Still, if his friends would like to have the opinion of a stranger concerning him, I think he will make a success here in one way or another. He has spirit and persistence. The only trouble is that he has too much hello about him."

Later that evening, Twain and the youth from Kalamazoo crossed paths at one of the weekly receptions held by Speaker of the House Schuyler

Colfax. The young man's enthusiasm had not dimmed. Twain recalled, "[I]f anybody was serenely and entirely at home in that brilliant gathering, and equal in all respects to the occasion, it was Kalamazoo, I think. He shouldered his way through the throng to shake hands with me, and I knew by the cheery tone of his voice that he had forgotten his anger and regarded me in the light of a cherished old acquaintance, when he said, 'Hello, old Smarty! In about an hour and a half, that fellow was acquainted with everybody in the house."

For both the young and ambitious office seeker from Kalamazoo and the young and ambitious polymath humorist-journalist-lecturer-author Twain, Speaker Colfax's weekly Friday receptions were a place to make introductions, seek favors and be seen by the women of the city. In late February 1868, the *National Intelligencer*, which Twain called a "staid old journal that regularly comes out in the most sensational and aggressive manner, every morning, with news it ought to have printed the day before," gave a short review of one of Speaker Colfax's receptions: "The spacious parlors were again thronged last evening, on the occasion of his weekly reception, with a most brilliant assemblage, composed, as usual, of official dignitaries of every branch of the Government, members of the *Corps Diplomatique*, and an unusually large number of distinguished strangers. Mr. Colfax received his many visitors in a most pleasing manner, introducing them to his accomplished mother and sister with that courtesy and urbanity which made all feel at ease. These agreeable reunions will be continued during the month of March."

Nearly forty years after his days as a capital correspondent, Twain found himself rummaging through "the pocket of one of those ancient memorandum-books of mine." Revealing the deep sense of tragedy Twain held with him his entire life, he dictated in an autobiographical sketch that "both the paper and the ink are yellow with the bitterness that I felt in that old day when I clipped it out to preserve it and brood over it and grieve about it." Twain read the excerpt, which described him in its entirety without mentioning its source: the pioneering Emily Edson Briggs, who wrote under the *nom de plume* of Olivia.

In *The Olivia Letters*, published in 1906, Briggs collected some of her choice Washington correspondence, including the item Twain ruminated on. With the headline "SPEAKER COLFAX. His Affection For His Mother—Other Characteristics" and datelined March 2, 1868, Briggs opened, "The season of Lent has folded its soft, brooding wings over the weary devotees of fashion in Washington. Luxuriant wrappers, weak tea, and soft-boiled eggs have succeeded the Eugenie trains, chicken salad, and all those delicious fluids that are supposed

While in Washington, Twain earned the praise of Speaker of the House Schuyler Colfax for his toast to women at the Washington Correspondents' Club dinner and later attended a reception at Colfax's home on Lafayette Square. *Library of Congress.*

to brace the human form divine." Briggs continued, "But as hardy as native flowers defy the chilly frost, so Speaker Colfax's hospitable doors swing upon their noiseless hinges once a week, and the famous house known as the 'Sickles Mansion' becomes a bee-hive, swarming, overflowing with honeyed humanity."

Among the civilization in attendance was Mark Twain, whom Briggs captured thusly:

Mark Twain, the delicate humorist, was present; quite a lion, as he deserves to be. Mark is a bachelor, faultless in taste, whose snowy vest is suggestive of endless quarrels with Washington washer-women; but the heroism of Mark is settled for all time, for such purity and smoothness were never seen before. His lavender gloves might have been stolen from some Turkish harem, so delicate were they in size; but more likely—anything else were more likely than that. In form and feature, he bears some resemblance to the immortal Nasby; but whilst Petroleum is brunette to the core, Twain is golden, amber-hued, melting blonde.

NEWSPAPER CORRESPONDENTS' CLUB

During Mark Twain's stay in Washington, there were nine city newspapers and more than two dozen out-of-town sheets with offices in the capital. From these ranks, journalists and editors found themselves in the city competing with each other to break stories but also contending with each other for social status. Newspaper Row was not only where hard news and information was gathered but also where the latest talk in fashion and culture was discussed and exchanged. Journalists returning to Washington from New York and other cities were known to import the "latest dance" at the "first grand ball" as "state sociables" were deemed too formal. Although Twain did not spend much of his time on the Row while in Washington, when the last of the buildings was razed in the late 1920s, he was listed in the *New York Times* as one of its famous alums. That Twain was a capital correspondent of consequence respected by his fellow journalists while in Washington is without question. Perhaps more feared than loved, Twain was in the city less than a month when he received an invitation to speak at a meeting of his peers.

"The Correspondents' Club have threatened to call me out for a speech for the benefit of their widows & orphans," Twain wrote Frank Fuller on December 13, 1867. Three days earlier, Twain wrote his family, "I am

The floor tiles and mirrors in the Senate Press Gallery were there when Twain was a capital correspondent. This view of the anteroom, which looks much the same today, was taken from *Harper's Monthly Magazine*. *Author's collection*.

writing a lecture—have half promised to deliver it b for [*sic*] the Newspaper Correspondents' Club here after the holidays—maybe I may—& I may not." Twain apparently attended a social function the second week of December during which he was asked to address an upcoming banquet. In his Washington letter to the *Daily Alta California* with a dateline of December 17, he retells the details with a flair: "I was at a dinner in the early part of the week, given by Mr. Henry D. Cook, to the Newspaper Correspondents' Club of Washington, where Ben. Perly Poore, a noted writer, said something which gave offence to General Boynton, late of the Army but now of the press, and yesterday the parties quarreled in the ante-room of the House reporters' gallery. A duel was talked of all day, but I hear to-night that Mr. Poore has apologized. It is a great pity. I never have seen a dead reporter."

According to the editors of the Mark Twain Papers, "The Washington Correspondents' Club, an association of journalists writing about Washington newspapers elsewhere, was founded in February 1867." The organization held its second annual banquet at 7:00 pm in Welcker's Restaurant on Saturday, January 11, 1868. Thirty-seven journalists and nine guests attended. Twain was ready for the occasion. Writing in the *Daily Alta California* with a dateline of January 11, Twain noted, "The Newspaper Correspondents' Club will have its annual banquet this evening, and a royal affair it will be. The boys have been making great preparations for it for some time. They tell me I am expected to respond to the regular toast to Woman. I don't care whether I am expected or not—I shall respond anyhow. It is my best hold. On all occasions, whenever woman is mentioned, I am ready to make a statement."

According to the *Evening Star* of January 13, 1868, the president of the club and Twain's one-time housemate, George Adams, part owner of the *Washington Evening Star* and Washington correspondent of the *New York World*, rose at about 10:00 pm to congratulate current members, remember fallen ones and recognize some of the earliest Washington correspondents. Adams, the presiding officer, then opened the floor for the "Club to speak for itself to the vast constituency which it represents." Twain, as planned, responded to the twelfth toast, "Woman: The Pride of the Professions, and the Jewel of Ours."

"I do not know why I should have been singled out to receive the greatest distinction of the evening, for so the office of replying to the toast to women has been regarded in every age," Twain said, as reported by the *Star*. "I do not know why I have received this distinction unless it be that

I am a trifle less homely than the other members of the club. But be this as it may, Mr. President, I am proud of the position, and you could not have chosen any one who would have accepted it more gladly or labored with a heartier good-will to do the subject justice than I. Because, sir, I love the sex." This elicited much laughter. Twain continued, "I love all the women, sir, irrespective of age or color. Human intelligence cannot estimate what we owe to woman, sir. She sews on our buttons, she mends or clothes, she ropes us in at the church fairs, she confide[s] in us, she tells us whatever she can find out about the little private affairs of the neighbors, she gives us a piece of her mind sometimes—and sometime all of it—she soothes our aching brows, she bears our children—ours as a general thing." Building toward his punch line, Twain said, "In all the relations of life, sir, it is but just and a graceful tribute to woman to say of her that she is a brick."

After mentioning a cadre of notable woman including Joan of Arc, Elizabeth Cady Stanton, Desdemona, Cleopatra, "Mother Eve" and George Washington's mother, who "raised a boy that could not lie" although "[i]t might have been different with him if he had belonged to a newspaper correspondents' club," Twain put the finishing touches on his remarks: "Not any here will refuse to drink her health right cordially in the bumper of wine, for each and everyone one of us has personally known, and loved, and honored, the very best one of them all—his own mother!" Writing to his mother, Jane Lampton Clemens, and family at two o'clock in the morning on January 14, 1868, with an enclosure of the *Star* article with his comments, Twain reported, "Speaker Colfax said [it] was the best dinner-table speech he ever heard at a banquet."

In a letter to the *Daily Alta California*, Twain revealed how the event was able to run into the wee hours of the night:

> *At 12 midnight, it was announced from the chair that the Sabbath was come, and that a due regard for the Christian character of our country demanded that the festivities should now come to an abrupt termination. The regular toasts were not finished yet. The fun was at its zenith. Here was a scrape. How would you have gotten out of it? I will tell how we managed it, and it will be worth your while to lay the information away for private use hereafter. It was gravely moved and as gravely seconded and carried, "That we do now discontinue the use of Washington time and adopt the time of San Francisco!" And then we bowled along as serenely as ever. We gained about three hours and a half by the operation! How is that*

for ingenuity? It was easy sailing after that. When we had used up all the San Francisco time and got to crowding Sunday again, we took another vote and adopted Hong Kong time. I suppose we would have been going west yet if the champagne had not given out.

CHAPTER 11

The Folklore of General Washington's Body Servant

Proceed, great chief, with virtue on thy side / Thy ev'ry action let the Goddess guide / A crown, a mansion, and a throne that shine / With gold unfading, Washington! Be thine.
—Phyllis Wheatley, 1775

When General Washington was on his deathbed, he rolled his eyes and said, "Forever keep the niggers down." This bit of psuedo-history passing from generation to generation is accepted as undoubtedly true by many, if not most, of the colored people over a wide area.
—"Folk-Lore Jottings in the District of Columbia," Journal of American Folklore, *1880*

[I]n the United States and the West Indies, the Negroes are humorous; they are filled with laughter and delicious chuckling. They enjoy themselves; they enjoy jokes; they perpetrate them on each other and on white folk.
—W.E.B. Du Bois, 1943

As a young boy in the border state of Missouri, Mark Twain grew up around slaves. At a young age, he internalized the folkways and folklore of black folk, sitting at rapt attention, elbow to elbow with black and white children during the storytelling sessions of slaves on his uncle's farm. "All the negroes were friends of ours, and with those of our own age we were in effect comrades," Twain wrote in 1907. "I say in effect, using the phrase as a modification. We were comrades, and yet not comrades; color and condition interposed a subtle line which both parties were conscious of and which rendered complete fusion impossible." The white urchins and enslaved children, equally, had a "faithful and affectionate good friend, ally and adviser in 'Uncle Dan'l,' a middle-aged slave whose head was the best one in the negro quarter, whose sympathies were wide and warm, and whose heart was honest and simple and knew no guile." Twain acknowledged that although he had not seen Uncle Dan'l for "more than a half a century," through the man's "spirituality I have had his welcome company a good part of the time." The memories of Uncle Dan'l had served Twain "well these many, many years," as Twain based characters on him and staged him in books. On his uncle's farm, Twain acquired his "strong liking for his race and my appreciation of certain of its fine qualities. This feeling and this estimate have stood the test of sixty years and more and suffered no impairment."

As a child, Twain accepted slavery as the status quo: "In my schoolboy days, I had no aversion to slavery. I was not aware that there was anything wrong about it. No one arraigned it in my hearing; the local papers said nothing against it; the local pulpit taught us that God approved it; that it was a holy thing, and that the doubter need only look in the Bible if he wished to settle his mind—and then the texts were read aloud to us to make the matter sure; if the slaves themselves had an aversion to slavery, they were wise and said nothing."

When Twain came to Washington City in late November 1867, he found himself back in the South after spending more than half a decade removed in Nevada Territory, California, present-day Hawaii, overseas and New York. In Washington, an old slave city, some of the stories Twain had heard and remembered from his childhood returned to him. One of these tales was the half-fact/half-fiction legend of the near-immortal black body servant of General George Washington. Written and published by Twain while in Washington City, "General Washington's Negro-Body Servant: A Biographical Sketch" has seemingly evaded intensive investigative scholarship.

Most likely composed in early December 1867 and published in the February 1868 edition of the *Galaxy*, the article was included in collections of Twain's writings during his life. It is by no means an obscure writing, nor one published after his death. Twain personally dismissed it as "a stupid article," and in advance of its publication, the *Evening Star* remarked it "to be provocative of levity." The story nevertheless hit at the heart of Washington's secret history and its black folklore, a folklore Twain was raised on.

Much has been written about Twain and race. His classic novel *Adventures of Huckleberry Finn* has been equally hailed as a subversive and ingenious undercutting of southern racism or decried as nothing more than a stereotype-perpetuating minstrel. In the early 1990s, scholar Shelley Fisher Fishkin posited that Huck Finn and his vernacular was, in fact, constructed on a black child. When *Adventures of Huckleberry Finn* was first published in the United States in 1885, it was banned—not because of the prominent use of a derogatory term for black folks, but because of fears that the uncouth and uncivilized Huck would have a derogatory effect on impressionable children. In recent years, a much-publicized edition of the book was published that replaced the more than two hundred uses of the antebellum pejorative racial epithet "nigger" with "slave." Editorials across the country were more often than not critical, without considering the motivation for the decision: not to haphazardly dilute Twain's story, but to make the book more accessible and acceptable so that it would be widely read.

Twain's literary talent was using the specific to illustrate larger social issues; he did not indulge in broad-based observations, but on the granular. "As a novelist, Mark Twain had little to say about the social and economic conditions of blacks in the postbellum South," Arthur Petitt writes in *Mark Twain and the South.* "He was a man of letters, not a sociologist; his interest focused on individuals, not on classes." From his decades of support of the Jubilee Singers to gracing the stage with Booker T. Washington, Twain "did not undertake special pleading for the negro cause; he only prepared the way with cheerfulness," according to his biographer. Nearly forgotten in the Twain canon, "General Washington's Negro-Body Servant" is a cryptic tale that echoes back to both Twain's childhood and to the surreptitious past of Washington City, where a man widely believed to be General Washington's body servant died within months of receiving his wartime pension at an age of more 110.

"Had the National Capital remained in Philadelphia, upon free soil, amid its loyal and national tendencies, had it breathed the air and heard the peaceful voice of the Society of Friends instead of the angry clamor of the Washington fire-eaters, some solution of the slave question might have been reached far short of rebellion, bloodshed and assassination," said Frederick Douglass in a public address delivered in the months before and after the country's centennial celebration. "[W]ho are the people of Washington and of the District of Columbia, the people who have given to the place its peculiar tone and character? The answer is, as already intimated, that they are mainly the old slaveholding stock of Virginia and Maryland." Before the war, they "lived in fine houses, rode in fine carriages, had fine old wines in their cellars, and knew how to give fine and sparkling champagne suppers. Judging from the social influence, they were a charming community of gentlemen and ladies." Their means of "revenue were slavery and the government."

The social system of Washington was turned on its head with "the suppression of the rebellion and the abolition of slavery, the prestige of Virginia has vanished and her glory has departed." In her place, the city was inundated with runaway slaves from Maryland, Virginia and other places farther South during and after the war. In April 1862, Washington City became the only place in the entire country that provided for compensated emancipation. The "first freed" were now de-facto members of the "self-reliant negro community," which numbered more than eleven thousand free black persons compared to just over three thousand slaves within Washington's city limits in 1860. At the outbreak of the war, there were more than sixty thousand whites in the city.

"As a class, the people of Washington, descendants of the old families, are very easily distinguished from people of the North, and West, and the East. The difference, however, between them and others, is not so easily described and defined as perceived. It is general rather than special," said Douglass, an acquaintance of Twain's (whose father-in-law, Jervis Langdon, had aided Douglass's flight from slavery in September 1838). "One of the peculiarities of the old Washington families will strike the ears of all educated people from the North. They will have something of the Negro in their speech, and many of them have it very strong. Even where there is much culture and refinement, there is often in their speech a tinge of the Negro's slovenly pronunciation. Born and reared among Negro slaves, learning their first songs and stories from their lips, they have naturally enough adopted the Negro's manner of using his vocal organs. I gather from this fact the small consolation that, if the blacks are too low to learn from the white, the whites are not too high to learn from the blacks, and further that the contact with ignorance promotes ignorance." Mark Twain was not above learning from black folk and calling out ignorance wherever and whenever he saw it.

John Cary: General Washington's Body Servant

In 1840, a member of the U.S. Marshal's office in Washington City enumerated John Cary under "FREE COLORED PERSONS" for the sixth decennial United States Census. For his age, Cary had two distinctive markings, one in the second column for "10 & under 24" and one in the last column for "100 & upwards." Cary's age was self-reported and recorded as being minimally 110 years old. The 1840 census was the first in which the age of Revolutionary War pensioners was asked.

In late January 1843, Cary's name appeared in a small notice reprinted in newspapers across the country. "Body Servant of Gen. Washington" was the short subhead. "On motion of Mr. Briggs, a resolution was adopted instructing the Committee on Revolutionary Pensions to inquire into the expediency of allowing a pension to John Cary, who says that he was the body servant of General Washington and was present with him at the defeat of Braddock [during the French and Indian War] and the surrender of Cornwallis [in 1781], and that he is 112 years old." On February 25, 1843, the *Radical*, published out of Pike County, Missouri, ran a story on Cary on its front page. "Gen. Washington's Body Servant" was the familiar subhead, quite possibly seen and discussed throughout the state of Missouri, reaching the ears of seven-year-old Samuel Clemens. "Mr. Taliaferro, from the Committee on Revolutionary Pensions in Congress, reported a bill allowing a pension to John Cary, a free colored man." The story gave similar biographical details of previous stories and concluded, "Thus the bill was read twice and committed to the Committee of the Whole on the State of the Union."

Four months later, on June 2, 1843, Cary died. He was believed to be 114 years old, according to *Nile's National Register*. "This is the same 'OLD JOHN,'" the *Register* reminded, "of whom some notice was taken in the *Intelligencer* last winter when a joint resolution was pending before congress to grant him a pension." According to the article, Cary "was born of African parents in Westmoreland [C]ounty, Virginia, in August 1729, two years and a half before the birth of GENERAL WASHINGTON, and in the same county. Had he lived two months longer, he would have reached the full age of 114 years. He accompanied Gen. WASHINGTON as his personal servant in the old French War and was with him in the battle-field on the Monongahela in July 1755, where Gen. Braddock was defeated and slain and where WASHINGTON, by his ability and prudence, covered the retreat and saved the remnant of the British army and laid the foundation of his future military fame."

The article continued:

In the war of the revolution, John followed to the camp and to the field his old commander, sometimes as a personal attendant and sometimes in the ranks of the army, and continued with him till the termination of hostilities. When retiring from the army, GENERAL WASHINGTON presented "Old John" with a military coat, the same which the general had worn at the siege of Yorktown, as a token of his approbation and esteem. This coat John carefully preserved as a sacred memento; and though in his old age reduced to extreme poverty, no money could ever tempt him to part with the coat. He wore it as a dress coat till within the last fifteen years of his life, and he left it as his richest earthly treasure.

Following the revolution and the founding of the United States, Cary "resided for several years in Westmoreland [C]ounty, where he became a devout member of the Baptist Church. Thence he moved to this place, and for the last twenty-eight years of his life was a member of the First Baptist Church" in Washington City. Until his last breath, Cary "was ardent in his patriotism and attachment to his country's father, the great WASHINGTON. He was still more ardent in his piety and devotion to GOD, his Eternal Father and Redeemer. His life was unstained, and his death was unclouded. He met without dread the King of Terrors and passed the vale of death without alarm."

Cary's death was widely reported throughout the region at the time. As late as 1858, his death was published in a national chronology of "memorable persons." It was well within reason to speculate that when Mark Twain reached Washington City in late November 1867, returning to the South, John Cary's memory was not forgotten.

BILLY LEE: GENERAL WASHINGTON'S BODY SERVANT

As Henry Wiencek presents in *An Imperfect God: George Washington, His Slaves, and the Creation of America*, the attitude of the founding father of our country toward slavery evolved over his lifetime. By the time of his death, Washington had made explicit provisions that "[u]pon the decease of my wife, it is my will and desire that all the slaves which I hold in my own right shall receive their freedom." Washington made this testament without the knowledge of his family. One slave, William "Billy" Lee, did not to have to wait for Martha's death.

William "Billy" Lee is believed to be captured on canvas alongside Washington and his family in at least two paintings, if not more, and was

George and Martha Washington and her two grandchildren around a table on which there is a map of Washington City, and an African American servant, William Lee, in background. Painting by Edward Savage (1761–1817). *Library of Congress.*

painted in portrait by Charles Wilson Peale in 1792. In John Trumbull's 1780 painting of George Washington, Lee is to Washington's left atop a horse; in Edward Savage's 1796 painting, *The Washington Family* (which is on display at the National Gallery of Art in Washington), Lee stands attentively as Washington, his wife and two step-grandchildren review a map of the future capital city.

According to historian Paul Leicester Ford, writing in 1898 in *The True George Washington*, "'Billy' was purchased by Washington in 1768 for sixty-eight pounds and fifteen shillings and was his constant companion during the war, even riding after his master at reviews." Ford continued:

> *In 1784, Washington told his Philadelphia agent that, "The mulatto fellow, William, who has been with me all the war, is attached (married, he says) to one of his own color, a free woman, who during the war was also of my family. She has been in an infirm condition for some time, and I had conceived that the connexion* [sic] *between them has ceased; but I am mistaken it seems; they are both applying to get her here, and tho' I never wished to see her more, I cannot refuse his request (if it can be complied*

with on reasonable terms), as he has served me faithfully for many years. After premising this much, I have to beg the favor of you to procure her a passage to Alexandria."

In 1785, while Washington was surveying a tract of land, William fell and broke his knee-pan, "which put a stop to my surveying; and with much difficulty I was able to get him to Abington, being obliged to get a sled to carry him on, as he could neither walk, stand or ride." From this injury, Lee never quite recovered, yet he started to accompany his master to New York in 1789, only to give out on the road. He was left at Philadelphia, and Lear wrote to Washington's agent that "The President will thank you to propose it to Will to return to Mount Vernon when he can be moved with safety—but if he is still anxious to come on here the President would gratify him, altho' he will be troublesome. He has been an old faithful Servant, this is enough for the President to gratify him in every reasonable wish."

In his will, Washington singled out Lee, who was granted "immediate freedom or, if he should prefer it (on account of the accidents which have befallen him and which have rendered him incapable of walking or of any active employment), to remain in the situation he now is, it shall be optional in him to do so. In either case, however, I allow him an annuity of thirty dollars during his natural life which shall be independent of the victuals and cloaths [*sic*] he has been accustomed to receive; if he chuses [*sic*] the last alternative, but in full with his freedom, if he prefers the first, and this I give him as a testimony of my sense of his attachment to me and for his faithful services during the Revolutionary War." Lee died in 1828 at Mount Vernon.

By factual accounts and legislation, Billy Lee and John Cary were General Washington's body servants. How many more body servants did Washington have? In 1858, a newspaper out of Wheeling, Virginia (which would later become West Virginia), reported the death of one of Washington's body servants. "An unusual feature," reported the *Wheeling Daily Intelligencer*, "however, is that he went with his later-day master to the Mexican war." The joke was far from over. "AND YET ANOTHER" was the headline in the Ohio newspaper, the *Anti-Slavery Bugle*, on August 6, 1859, after one of Washington's body servants, "who bears the aristocratic name of Richard Stanhope," was reported to have passed. "It has been computed there is in existence at the present time wood enough of the true cross to build a battleship of the largest size. It would be interesting to lovers of the curious to have taken a census of the servants of Gen. Washington—the dead, as well as the living," suggested the abolitionist rag. "The newspapers bring us an account every little while of some one—generally a 'body servant'—who has not before been counted. We forget how many slaves it is said the King of Ashantee has in his bodyguard, but think not less than a thousand. These slaves of Gen. Washington—or servants, we should perhaps say—that phrase being better suited to delicate and fastidious ears: these servants of Gen. Washington, we were about to remark, will outnumber those of the King of Ashantee unless a speedy stop is put to their unnatural increase." Prophesying Twain's satirical article nine years later and future historiographies, the paper noted, "We have no question but that some brother editor who chronicles the close of the Twentieth Century will mention in that connection the remarkable fact that a former body servant of Gen. Washington is yet living in that vicinity. Who will say that longevity is not increasing, at least among the servant and body servants of Gen. Washington? We have read of the tomb wherein reposed 'The Last of the Capulets,' but our imagination cannot delude us into the belief that we shall live long enough to hear of the demise of the last of Washington's servants."

Mark Twain's Forgotten Sketch

Appearing as his first contribution to the *Galaxy* magazine in February 1868, "General Washington's Negro Body-Servant: A Biographical Sketch," is a restrained and coded strike by Twain at the "infamous old fraud." In black communities throughout the country, elderly men claimed the elevated status of being a body servant to George Washington, and newspapers editors perpetuated the fraud. "Though most slaves died at younger ages than most whites, fanciful stories regarding the unbelievable longevity of an occasional slave appeared in Missouri newspapers" in the years leading up to the Civil War. It is likely that Twain first read and heard these tales as a child. In Washington City only a matter of days, he mentions the story of the recurring elderly body servant in a draft of a play he enclosed to his friend Charles Henry Webb. "He comes from the first families of this place & his uncle has been post master once & his grandfather was a Home Guard in the Revolutionary War," Twain wrote. "He knowed the nigger that was body-servant servant to Genl. Washington. Notwithstanding that that nigger in a bogus form keeps turning up every year & dying in the newspapers at the most cussedest unearthly ages that ever even Methuselah heard of, but not genuine & not to be relied on." He would revisit the phenomenon in a matter of days in an attempt to write its epithet.

Twain opened his biographical sketch of General Washington's body servant by declaring, "The stirring part of this celebrated colored man's life properly began with his death—that is to say, the notable features of his biography begin with the first time he died. He had been little heard of up to that time, but since then we have never ceased to hear of him; we have never ceased to hear of him at stated, unfailing intervals. His was a most remarkable career, and I have thought that its history would make a valuable addition to our biographical literature." Posing as an irreverent historical detective, Twain "carefully collated the materials for such a work, from authentic sources, and here present them to the public. I have rigidly excluded from these pages everything of a doubtful character, with the object in view of introducing my work into the schools for the instruction of the youth of my country."

Ignoring the factual story of John Cary or Billy Lee, Twain claimed, "The name of the famous body-servant of General Washington was George," who "[a]fter serving his illustrious master faithfully for half a century, and enjoying throughout this long term his high regard and confidence, it became his sorrowful duty at last to lay that beloved master to rest in his peaceful grave by the Potomac." In 1799, ten years after Washington's death, his body servant died for the first time, as was reported by the *Boston Gazette*, Twain claimed. "George, the favorite body-servant of the lamented Washington, died in Richmond, Va., last Tuesday, at the ripe age of 95 years. His intellect was unimpaired and his memory tenacious up to within a few minutes of his decease. He was present at the second installation of Washington as President and also at his funeral and distinctly remembered all the prominent incidents connected with those noted events."

For the next sixteen years, there was silence, says Twain, "until May 1825, at which time he died again." This time a Philadelphia broadsheet chronicled the "sad occurrence." The paper read, "At Macon, Ga., last week, a colored man named George, who was the favorite body-servant of General Washington, died at the advanced age of 95 years. Up to within a few hours of his dissolution, he was in full possession of all his faculties and could distinctly recollect the second installation of Washington, his death and burial, the surrender of Cornwallis, the Battle of Trenton, the griefs and hardships of Valley Forge, etc. Deceased was followed to the grave by the entire population of Macon."

However, Twain wrote "[o]n the Fourth of July, 1830, and also of 1834 and 1836, the subject of this sketch was exhibited in great state upon the rostrum of the orator of the day." (Reports of the Independence Day orations were likely imagined [and multiplied] by a satirical Twain. However, newspapers in Missouri did report in August 1853 that "General Washington's sole surviving slave, a male aged 124 years, was being transported to the World's Fair and put on display near a contribution box for the Washington Monument.") In November 1840, he died yet again:

> *The St. Louis "Republican" of the 25th of that month spoke as follows: ANOTHER RELIC OF THE REVOLUTION GONE. George, once the favorite body-servant of General Washington, died yesterday at the house of Mr. John Leavenworth, in this city, at the venerable age of 95 years. He was in the full possession of his faculties up to the hour of his death and distinctly recollected the first and second installations and death of President Washington, the surrender of Cornwallis, the battles of Trenton and Monmouth, the sufferings of the Patriot Army at Valley Forge, the proclamation of the Declaration of Independence, the speech of Patrick Henry in the Virginia House of Delegates, and many other old-time reminiscences of stirring interest. Few white men die lamented as was this aged negro. The funeral was very largely attended.*

Risen from the dead like Lazarus, or his mantle adopted by impersonators, body servants kept dying. Twain wrote, "During the next ten or eleven years, the subject of this sketch appeared at intervals at Fourth of July celebrations in various parts of the country and was exhibited upon the rostrum with flattering success." In the fall of 1855, the latest iteration of the obituary of General Washington's body servant was printed, this time in papers in California. Nine years later, in June 1864, was the "last time the subject of this sketch died," Twain said. "And until we learn the contrary, it is just to presume that he died permanently this time." Dying in Detroit, the "Cherished Remnant of the Revolution" was reportedly ninety-five years old but "could distinctly remember" events that happened more than a century ago, including "the landing of the Pilgrims."

Twain was exclamatory. "The faithful old servant is gone! We shall never see him more, until he turns up again. He has closed his long and splendid career of dissolution, for the present, and sleeps peacefully, as only they sleep who have earned their rest. He was in all respects a remarkable man. He held his age better than any celebrity that has figured in history; and the longer he lived, the stronger and longer his memory grew. If he lives to die again, he will distinctly recollect the discovery of America."

Confident in his collation of fictional source material, Twain wrote, "The above resume of his biography I believe to be substantially correct, although it is possible that he may have died once or twice in obscure places where the event failed of newspaper notoriety." An oddity or "fault" that Twain found in the narrative was that in "all notices of his death which I have quoted," Washington's body servant "uniformly and impartially died at the age of 95. This could not have been. He might have done that once, or maybe twice, but he could not have continued it indefinitely. Allowing that when he first died, he died at the age of 95, he was 151 years old when he died last, in 1864. But his age did not keep pace with his recollections. When he died the last time, he distinctly remembered the landing of the Pilgrims, which took place in 1620." The numbers did not add up. "He must have been about twenty years old when he witnessed that event; wherefore it is safe to assert that the body servant of General Washington was in the neighborhood of two hundred and sixty or seventy years old when he departed this life finally." As a child on his uncle's farm, Twain and his "comrades" believed that Aunt Hannah was one thousand years old. The young Twain was familiar with—and believed—claims of eternal black life.

Twain closed his article by letting his readers know that he had "waited a proper length of time to see if the subject of this sketch had gone from us reliably and irrevocably. I now publish his biography with confidence and respectfully offer it to a mourning Nation." With his frequent use of a postscript, Twain lamented:

> *I see by the papers that this infamous old fraud has just died again, in Arkansas. This makes six times that he is known to have died, and always in a new place. The death of Washington's body-servant has ceased to be a novelty; its charm is gone; the people are tired of it; let it cease. This well-meaning but misguided negro has now put six different communities to the expense of burying him in state and has swindled tens of thousands of people into following him to the grave under the delusion that a select and peculiar distinction was being conferred upon them. Let him stay buried for good now; and let that newspaper suffer the severest censure that shall ever, in all future time, publish to the world that General Washington's favorite colored body-servant has died again.*

From a survey of nineteenth-century newspapers made electronically accessible by the Library of Congress Chronicling America site, it appears Twain's story did not offer the last the word on this sensation. In September

1869, the *Cambria Freeman* out of Pennsylvania reported, "Gen. Washington's body-servant is dead again. He was a she this time—colored, and of the name of Mrs. Thurnea, and died in Kentucky at the age of a hundred and nineteen years. Adieu, once more, immortal fraud." Earlier that year, a paper reported that a "distinguished resident of Topeka, [Kansas] a colored citizen of African descent named Joshua Pickett, who was born on the Calhoun estate in South Carolina in 1733," had died. After briefly listing his "honorable occupation[s]," the article noted, "What is most singular of all, Joshua was never a body servant of Gen. Washington." In 1882, a Dallas paper reported under a subhead of "The Ungrateful Republic" that "an aged colored man who claims to have been the body servant of General Washington" was sent to the workhouse. The year before, in Council Bluffs, Iowa, a hotel waiter named George Washington, who was a "second cousin to a step-sister of an acquaintance of one of General G. Washington's 'most trusted body servants,' came to an untimely end in that city recently," reported the *Indianapolis Ledger*. "He quarreled with his head-waiter, and the latter willfully, regardless of his 'noble ancestry,' shot him dead through the heart."

By the turn of the twentieth century, the joke was nearly spent, but it still showed signs of life. "Their Name Is Legion" headlined a paper in Minnesota in 1905, reprinting a story that had appeared in the *Houston Chronicle*. "The aged colored gentleman had applied for admission at the pearly gates. 'What was your business when on earth?' inquired St. Peter. 'Body servant to Gen. Washington, sah.' 'Oh, well, you want to go to that lower gate,' said St. Peter, not unkindly. 'You see, body servants of Gen. Washington got so numerous that we roped off a nice, roomy section where they could all be together. You'll find 'em all there.' And the aged Ethiopian tottered away."

Even if the joke was near its conclusion in print, nearly half a century after Mark Twain wrote of the folklore of black Washingtonians, it remained in currency and peddled within the city's black community. "Until recently, there was a very old negro in Washington who said he had been the slave and body servant of General Washington and remembered the General very well," reported the *New York Sun* in 1913. The elderly man remembered when Washington "took that hack at the cherry tree."

The year before, columnist Roy K. Moulton alleged to have had an encounter in Washington City with not an aged body servant but a youthful one:

> *There is one unique institution in Washington, and I must speak of it briefly or explode. The institution referred to is George Washington's*

personal body servant. He is a numerous and ubiquitous institution and can be found in the most surprising walks of life. The first one I discovered was running the elevator in our hotel. He is the only surviving body servant of George Washington. It is unnecessary to prove it on him, for he is perfectly willing to admit it. There are believed to be eighty-five or one hundred other only surviving body servants of George Washington in this city, but they are said to be scattered about through other portions of the South quite discriminately. I have met twenty or twenty-five only surviving body servants, and I have been here only a short time, and will probably meet the rest of them before I leave. George Washington must have been surrounded by a standing army of body servants.

Out of that army, Moulton singled out a young man running the hotel elevator in his column:

He told us about it while we were going from the first floor to the second. Personal body servants of the late George Washington lose no time. We sighed deeply and handed him $1 in grateful appreciation of services rendered the truthful George. There may be something in environment, but none of George's well-known truthfulness ever soaked into any of his body servants. The body servant running the elevator looked to be about forty years old.

"What's your name?"

"Abraham Lincoln Jones," he replied with a face as innocent of guile as that of a standpat congressman making a speech in his home district.

"Ah ha! If you are old enough to have been George Washington's body servant, how could your name be Abraham Lincoln?"

Ever ready for pressure under fire, Jones replied, "Well, boss, you see it's dis yere way. I 'herited it from my fathah and he 'herited it from my gran'fatha, so I have got de job now. I am Washington's body servant. My fathah done tole me so. My grand'fathah thought of it first and held de job till he die, den he turn it over to my fathah an' he turn it over to me. My son will be de personal body servant of Marse Washington in a few years now."

Moulton was satisfied, writing, "There was no argument to be used against that. It runs in the family like cauliflower ears, pug noses or wooden legs, and the only thing to do is to hand over the price. When we see a personal body servant of George Washington loom up on the horizon now we simply dig and ask no questions."

An 1822 oil painting of Yarrow Mamout by James Alexander Simpson (1805–1880). A Charles Wilson Peale painting of Mamout was misidentified as being General Washington's body servant as late as the 1990s. *Collection of Peabody Room, DC Public Library.*

In Mark Twain's 1881 book *The Prince and the Pauper*, he writes a preface that could just as easily apply to a book on the legend of General Washington's body servant: "I will set down a tale as it was told to me by one who had it of his father, which latter had it of his father, this last having in like manner had it of his father—and so on, back and still back, three hundred years and more, the fathers transmitting it to the sons and so preserving. It may be history, it may be only a legend, a tradition. It may have happened, it may not have happened: but it COULD have happened. It may be that the wise and the learned believed it in the old days; it may be that only the unlearned and the simple loved it and credited it."

CHAPTER 12

Exit Stage West

Impeachment has gone beyond newspaper discussion.
—*John Russell Young,* New York Tribune, *February 26, 1868*

"Mark Twain"—Clemens—has left Washington for California to make arrangements for the publication of his work.
—Evening Star, *March 9, 1868*

In the thick of the Senate's impeachment trial of Andrew Johnson, the biggest newspaper story of the year, Mark Twain skipped town. In Washington, he had succeeded in establishing a larger and more notable name for himself and unexpectedly secured a book-publishing contract with a reputable house. Two separate events hastened his quick departure from the city in early March 1868. First, in order to move forward on his contract with the American Publishing Company to complete *The Innocents Abroad*, he would have to travel to San Francisco to negotiate the copyright and ownership of his published letters with the owners of the *Daily Alta California*. Secondly, there was increasingly no hope that Twain could secure an appointment for his brother, Orion, who by late February had similarly abandoned the idea.

"I am glad you do not want the clerkship, for that Patent Office is in such a muddle that there would be no security for the permanency of a place in it," Twain wrote Orion on February 21, 1868. "The same remark will apply to all offices here, now, & no doubt will till the close of the present

THE REPORTERS' GALLERY OF THE HOUSE OF REPRESENTATIVES, WASHINGTON, D.C.—SKETCHED BY THEODORE R. DAVIS.—[SEE NEXT PAGE.]

"The Reporter's Gallery of the House of Representatives, Washington, D.C.—Sketched by Theodore R. Davis." *Harper's Weekly*, March 7, 1868. Twain left Washington hours after this print was published. *Library of Congress.*

administration. Any man who holds a place here, now, stands prepared at all times to vacate it." At the time of the letter, Orion was setting type for the *Missouri Democrat*. Twain offered faint praise for Orion, writing, "You are doing now exactly what I wanted you to do a year ago." In the next line, Twain penned an epigram that was as true of his brother, who died in 1897, as it was of him: "We chase phantoms half the days of our lives." During his transitory stretch in Washington, Twain saw up close and personal how

The National Hotel at Sixth and Pennsylvania Avenue around 1860. Originally opening as Gadsby's Hotel during Andrew Jackson's time, this was the site of one of Twain's tales of old Washington folklore. *Library of Congress.*

chasing after phantoms, or government claims and positions, could waste away entire lives.

First appearing in his Washington letter to the *Territorial Enterprise* on March 1, 1868, the story of "The Man Who Stopped at Gadsby's" was a tale that stuck with Twain, and he repeated it in full in his 1880 book *A Tramp Abroad.* Twain initially relates the story in his dispatch to the *Enterprise* in relation to a recently arrived office seeker in Washington pursuing appointment as the postmaster of San Francisco. He was the thirty-seventh person known to be chasing the position. "He is a good enough man and may get the place, but it will cost him more trouble and vexation than he is promising himself, no doubt," Twain writes. With the Senate and President Johnson at odds, the man was in a precarious position. According to Twain, "He says he can't see that there is anything to be done but get the President to appoint and the Senate to ratify. Certainly that is all, truly enough. It was all that was to be accomplished by the thirty-six. He says he means to show the President what the Pacific coast papers say about him, and he means also

139

to tell him all about how the Post Office has heretofore been managed and how he would improve that management the moment he got into office." However, the man was unlikely to secure the position, Twain estimated, because "he don't say he would swear by Andrew Johnson and labor for his behest alone—which is much more important. And he don't take into consideration that the moment he gets the President in his favor, the Senate will be down on him for it, and that if he gains the Senate's affections first, the President will be down on him."

Even after hearing the tale of the man who stayed at Gadsby's from Twain's friend Riley, the San Franciscan's naïveté held firm when he said he planned to stay in Washington but a week. "He says he don't care anything about making an extended stay in Washington—he only wants to get the appointment and look around the great public buildings a little, and then he is off," Twain wrote. The man had been warned, although Twain didn't think "he saw the point of it or not. It was a little story that has been related with great spirit many thousands of times to office seekers and claim-hunters who were only going to tarry a few days in Washington."

Twain wrote years later that he and his friend John Henry Riley had allegedly met the innocent office seeker and relayed the cautionary Gadsby's Hotel tale to him personally. One night, near midnight, Twain and Riley were coming down Pennsylvania Avenue "in a driving storm of snow when the flash of a street lamp fell upon a man who was eagerly tearing along in the opposite direction." On noticing Riley, the man stopped dead in his tracks. "My name is Lykins," the man said. "I'm one of the teachers of the high school—San Francisco. As soon as I heard the San Francisco postmastership was vacant, I made up my mind to get it—and here I am." Riley asked if the man had secured the position. "Well, not exactly got it, but the next thing to it," the man said. "I've brought a petition, signed by the Superintendent of Public Instruction, and all the teachers, and by more than two hundred other people. Now I want you, if you'll be so good, to go around with me to the Pacific delegation, for I want to rush this thing through and get along home." Riley, whom Twain admired as "the most self-possessed and solemnly deliberate person in the republic," responded to the man "in a voice which had nothing mocking in it—to an unaccustomed ear" by saying: "If the matter is pressing, you will prefer that we visit the delegation to-night."

The man answered with enthusiasm. "Oh, to-night, by all means! I haven't got any time to fool around. I want their promise before I go to bed—I ain't the talking kind, I'm the doing kind!" Riley cajoled Lykins, telling him, "[Y]ou've come to the right place for that." After considering the particulars of how Lykins and Riley could rapidly ensure the appointment would go through the next day before Lykins had to return to San Francisco, Riley asked, "You couldn't stay a day…well, say two days longer?"

Lykins responded emphatically, "Bless your soul, no! It's not my style. I ain't a man to go fooling around—I'm a man that does things, I tell you." The storm had picked up, "the thick snow blowing in gusts." Poised, Riley looked at Lykins and asked, "Have you ever heard about that man who put at Gadsby's once? But I see you haven't." Riley "backed Mr. Lykins against an iron fence, buttonholed him, fastened him, with his eye, like the Ancient Mariner, and proceeded to unfold his narrative as placidly and peacefully as if we were all stretched comfortably in a blossomy summer meadow instead of being persecuted by a wintry midnight tempest." Riley began to tell the tale: "It was in Jackson's time. Gadsby's was the principal hotel then." According to local historian John DeFerrari, "Originally founded in 1827 by John Gadsby, the National Hotel was located on Pennsylvania Avenue at 6th Street, NW. Gadsby, who had run Gadsby's Tavern in Alexandria in the 1790s, came to Washington in the early 1820s, taking over a tavern and hotel at 19th and I Streets, NW. That place was too small and out of the way, however, so in 1827, he purchased the row of federal townhouses on the northeast corner of Pennsylvania Avenue at 6th Street, NW, and combined them to form the hotel he called the National but which was more frequently known as Gadsby's Hotel in its early days." By the time Riley relayed the tale Gadsby's Hotel was only used in conversation by old Washingtonians. The National Hotel was its current name and known all around town for its telegraph office, right down the street from the Capitol. The story Riley spun was a cautionary tales from the early days of Washington City.

"Well, this man arrived from Tennessee about nine o'clock one morning, with a black coachmen and a splendid four-house carriage and an elegant dog, which he was evidently fond and proud of," Riley said. The man then "drove up before Gadsby's, and the clerk and the landlord and everybody rushed out to take charge of him; but he said 'Never mind,' and jumped out and told the coachman to wait." The man was in a rush and didn't have time for a meal. He had "only a little claim against the Government to collect, would run across the way to the Treasury and fetch the money, and then get right along back to Tennessee, for he was in a considerable hurry." Around eleven o'clock that night, the man returned to Gadsby's Hotel and took a bed and put his horses up, vowing to collect on his claim the next morning. According to Riley, this was January 3, 1834.

"Well, on the 5th of February, he sold the fine carriage and bought a cheap second-hand one—said it would answer just as well to take the money home in, and he didn't care for style," Riley continued. By August 11, the man from Tennessee sold a pair of his fine horses, leaving him two of the four he came to Washington with. He reasoned "there wasn't so much of his claim but he could lug the money home with a pair easy enough." On December 13, he sold another horse, and on February 17, 1835, "he sold the old carriage and bought a cheap second-hand buggy." On August 1, he sold the buggy, and on August 29 "he sold his coloured coachman." Eighteen months later, on February 15, 1837, he downgraded from his sulky to a saddle by reasoning that "horseback riding was what the doctor has always recommended." On April 9, 1837, he sold the saddle and alleged he could now ride back to Tennessee bareback.

Riley pressed on with his story: "On the 24th of April he sold his horse—said, 'I'm just 57 to-day, hale and hearty—it would be a pretty howdy-do for me to be wasting such a trip as that and such weather as this on a horse when there ain't anything in the world so splendid as a tramp on foot through the fresh spring woods.'" The man would "make my dog carry my claim in a little bundle anyway, when it's collected. So to-morrow I'll be up bright and early, make my little old collection, and mosey off to Tennessee, on my own hind legs, with a rousing good-bye to Gadsby's." If only the man was so fortunate. On June 22, he sold his dog: "I'd a blamed sight rather carry the claim myself, it's a mighty sight safer; a dog's mighty uncertain in a financial way—always noticed it—well good-bye, boys—last call—I'm off for Tennessee with a good leg and a gay heart, early in the morning!"

The noise of the wind and the pelting of the snow filled the silence as Riley finished his story. An impatient Lykins asked, "Well?" Riley, according to Twain, said, "Well, that was thirty years ago." Riley was friendly with the "old patriarch. He comes every morning to tell me good-bye. I saw him an hour ago—he's off for Tennessee early to-morrow morning—as usual; said he calculated to get his claim through and be off before night-owls like me have turned out to bed. The tears were in his eyes, he was so glad he was going to see his old Tennessee and his friends once more." Again there was a silent pause. "That is all," Riley said. "Well, for the time of night and the kind of night, it seems to me the story was full long enough. But what's it all for?" asked Lykins.

"Oh, there isn't any particular point to it," Riley admitted. "Only, if you are not in too much of a hurry to rush off to San Francisco with that post-office appointment, Mr. Lykins, I'd advise you to 'put up at Gadsby's' for a spell and take it easy. Good-bye. God bless you!" With that, "Riley blandly turned on his heel and left the astonished school-teacher standing there, a musing and motionless snow image shining in the broad glow of the street-lamp." Orion, who sought through his younger brother a position as head of the Patent Office, like Lykins, never did obtain an appointment.

Writing to his family in the first week of February 1868, Twain revealed that, in fact, he had been in the running for the appointment of postmaster of San Francisco; that is, if he had wanted it. "Judge Field said if I wanted the place he could Pledge me the President's appointment—& Senator Conness said he would *guarantee* me the Senate's confirmation. It was a great temptation, but it would render it impossible to fill my book contract, & I had to drop the idea." Twain revealed that California senator John Conness "offers me my choice out of five influential California offices—now some day or other I shall *want* an office & then, just my luck, I can't get it, I suppose. They want to send me abroad, as a Consul or a Minister. I said I didn't want any of the pie. God knows I am mean enough & lazy enough, now, without being a foreign consul."

CHAPTER 13

George Alfred Townsend: A Forgotten Man of Letters

Tell it not in Gath, publish it not in the streets of Askelon.
—2 Samuel 1:20, King James Bible

During Mark Twain's 1867–68 winter sojourn in Washington City, he lodged in boardinghouses with a crowd of correspondents who every year henceforth until the early twentieth century would produce hundreds of thousands of words for newspapers, magazines, journals, biographies, dramas, novels, histories and school textbooks. The most prolific writer Twain shared a roof with while a capital correspondent was George Alfred Townsend, whose decades of daily newspaper columns for sheets throughout the country, fiction, poems, plays and detective work uncovering the history of Washington, lore of the Chesapeake Bay Watershed and the assassination of President Lincoln, among other curiosities and intrigues, have been today almost forgotten. Since Townsend's death in 1914, he has been the subject of only two biographies, while making brief cameos here and there in volumes on the history of Washington journalism and the press corps. More recently, James Swanson's best-selling work *Manhunt: The 12-Day Chase for Lincoln's Killer* has brought Townsend's two decades investigating the assassination back into focus. Believed to be the youngest Civil War correspondent, Townsend was the most prominent newsman of his era, although today he is almost overlooked but for historians who find his rich reportorial material is as fresh today as when it was first penned, or dictated, for the written record. Although only one letter is known to survive between Townsend and Twain, the two maintained an apparent friendship decades after they met as young bohemians in Washington City. They were larger-than-life contemporaries who shared similar characteristics of pugnacity, ostentatiousness and a commitment to a life of letters. While Twain left journalism for authorship shortly after leaving Washington City, Townsend, who wrote more than two dozen books, dedicated himself full force to journalism. Today, Twain is remembered and Townsend is largely overlooked.

Born on January 30, 1841, in Delaware, Townsend moved around frequently as a child within the upper Chesapeake watershed, depending on where his father, Stephen Townsend, an itinerant Methodist Minister, was called to preach. At fifteen, Townsend entered Central High School, a prestigious institution founded in Philadelphia in the 1820s, after previously attending Washington College in Chester County, Maryland. At sixteen, he published a magazine that drew the attention of a railroad executive followed by articles for his high school journal. Graduating from Central with a BA in January 1860, he secured a job with the *Philadelphia Inquirer* at a rate of six dollars a week when just nineteen years old. "When Townsend became a reporter in the city, it was not what he wanted, but he…did his work so well

that he was in request," writes biographer Ruthanna Hindes. "Townsend had always wanted to be a 'special' writer. When he started in newspaper work, there were very few correspondents. Because the papers he worked for had pecuniary enterprise, a man was never sent anywhere to report. He was furnished only with a free ticket and was expected to provide for his food and room." In 1861, the rival *Philadelphia Press* lured Townsend from the *Inquirer* with the offer of becoming city

George Alfred Townsend, circa 1865. *Gathland State Park, Maryland Department of Natural Resources.*

editor. During this time, he "rehabilitate[d] local reporting and editing" in the city and even wrote his first play, *The Bohemians*. "The whole first year of the Civil War passed by with Townsend doing nothing more than writing up local Philadelphia events for the *New York Herald*." Townsend was restless.

In April 1862, at the age of twenty-one, Townsend became a war correspondent. Hindes writes, "At the time, most of the news was described so carelessly that the correspondents were embroiled or confused with the commanders. Later, when the publishing of the correspondents' names became mandatory, the writers were put on their mettle and were more careful to be accurate and successful." Townsend embedded with George McClellan's Army of the Potomac and wrote an account of Cedar Mountain in General Pope's campaign in August 1862 for the *New York Herald*. That fall, Townsend apparently contracted the "Chickahominy Fever" and subsequently traveled to Europe, where he "lectured and wrote articles about the conflict" for London- and Edinburgh-based publications. By mid-1864, Townsend returned to America and took up editing and writing responsibilities for a collection of New York papers. Desiring to be where the action was, Townsend traveled down South to once again embed

Newspaper carts visited Civil War camps and the edge of battlefields, bringing news to the front. *Library of Congress*.

as a war correspondent. At the Battle of Five Forks on March 31, 1865, Townsend was the only correspondent present and broke the nationwide story. Receiving a direct account from General Philip Sheridan after the battle, Townsend "rode twenty miles to reach an army telegraph wire to send the news to the North that Sheridan had won the decisive victory that led to the adornment of Petersburg and Richmond, and certainly the end of the Civil War."

In Richmond, Townsend and Jerome B. Stillson reported on the "desolate condition of the former Confederate capital and stronghold" for the *New York World*. Upon hearing of the shooting of President Lincoln, Stillson and Townsend caught the first train to Washington. "Lincoln's assailant had been seen by many in the audience as he leapt from the presidential box onto the stage after the shooting and made his escape on a waiting horse," writes Jerry Shields. "Several had recognized him as actor John Wilkes Booth," whom Townsend had known "since his stint as drama editor for the *Philadelphia Press* four years earlier." Only a few weeks before the shooting, Townsend reportedly spoke with Booth "when he stopped over in Washington on his way to join Sheridan's army" in Virginia. Townsend "was thus in a unique position to write about this assassin, who was still being sought after escaping with an accomplice through southern Maryland on his way to Virginia." In memoirs compiled in 1913, Townsend recalled, "When I was twenty-four years old, Mr. Lincoln's murder I heard of in burning Richmond City and at Washington. I found Detective Police from everywhere, stimulated by the rewards, many of whom knew me from my police reporting days, and they gave me advance information. My Booth letters to the *New York World* were collected in a pamphlet which I saw before each member of the Military Court and found it quickly circulated at the Baltimore and Philadelphia new companies. When I called on the publisher, he began the usual process of bluffing the author, so I sold for $300 a copyright good the rest of my life." Over the next two decades, Townsend would continue to study and track down sources in the "historic crime."

In the fall of 1865, Townsend married Miss Bessie Evans Rhodes of Philadelphia. The newlyweds traveled abroad in 1866, and Townsend reported on the Austro-Prussian War for the *New York World*. Shortly after seeing the Paris Exhibition in the spring of 1867, Townsend returned to the United States and settled in Washington City. According to Hindes, Townsend settled in Washington to study government. "He wanted to find out how business was formed and advanced from bills to committees, committees to reports and reports to legislation. His idea was not a mercenary

Townsend's *nom de plume*, GATH, and favorite phrase, "The Pen Is Mightier Than the Sword," adorned thousands of cigar tins. *Gathland State Park, Maryland Department of Natural Resources.*

one." Townsend was "naturally an independent political writer, and his presence in Washington was instantly acknowledged. His vigor, diligence, versatile reading, his sweeping diction, which was occasionally let down to humor, made his audacity menacing in political writing." When he arrived in Washington, "he could find his way about almost as well as any native—such was the man."

With an established reputation as a journalist of the first rate, Townsend contracted to compose capital correspondence for the *Chicago Tribune, Cleveland Leader, Cincinnati Commercial* and other papers across the country. While Townsend's letters were "mainly occupied with politics and the advocating of Republicanism," they also included local discussions such as detailing the history of efforts to remove the capital from Washington. His stature continued to grow, and around this time, his chief *nom de plume* of "Gath" first appeared in print in the *Chicago Tribune.* According to Jerome Stillson, Townsend employed over twenty pen names throughout his career but was most commonly identified as Gath, including his appearance in an 1881 article in the *National Republican* that listed more than two dozen "literary pseudonyms," including "Mark Twain."

When telling of his memories in Washington, Twain would frequently mention Townsend, whom he lived with. In chapter forty of Townsend's 1873 classic, *Washington, Outside and Inside,* Townsend elevated Twain to the company of the most prominent literary men Washington could yet claim:

Art, Letters, and Bohemians at the Capital

Around the Capital of a great nation the artistic and literary spirits have always assembled, and this has been the case with Washington. It has been from the beginning of its history a place of resort for tourists and literary men, and a place of abode for journalists, scholars, and artists. The kindly Paulding was both Secretary of the Board of Navy Commissioners and Secretary of the Navy, and the air of the latitude of Washington appears in his style. William Wirt gave scarcely less time to literature in this District than he had given in Virginia. Robert Walsh, perhaps the founder of review literature in America, was educated at Georgetown and spent much of his life in Washington. Here Joel Barlow, the author of The Columbiad, *built himself a mansion in the Jeffersonian day. For many years the publishers of that most useful repository, now unhappily discontinued, issued* Niles Register *on Louisiana Avenue. Sparks, Irving, Kennedy, Poe, Legaré, Cooper, Motley, Bancroft, Ross Brown, and Mark Twain are amongst the hundreds of notable men who have at periods been tenants of the city. Here resided Schoolcraft, Stanley, Catlin, and others who have transmitted the wild Indian to wonder and fame. Here Peter Force, the pious book collector, lived until the Government took his library, and then died for employment and want of responsibility. The most influential novel in the world was published in monthly parts by Mrs. Stowe in a Washington newspaper. The diplomatic and official history of the country has been almost wholly edited and collected here, and the journalism of the country has been in great part learned here.*

TOWNSEND AND TWAIN SIT FOR BRADY'S CAMERA

In early February 1871, Twain was passing through Washington to check on the status of Jervis Langdon's (his deceased father-in-law) "lawsuit against Memphis, Tennessee, initiated in 1869, for non-payment of a five-

A photo taken by Mathew Brady showing Mark Twain (center), George Alfred Townsend (left) and David Gray (right). *Library of Congress.*

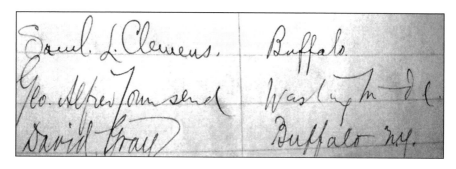

Brady's Register, LOT 11446-7, February 1871, denotes the sitting of Clemens, Townsend and Gray. *Library of Congress.*

hundred-thousand-dollar street paving bill." Back in the capital city, staying at the Ebbitt House at the corner of Fourteenth and F Streets NW, Twain reconnected with his former housemate Townsend. Twain, then an editor at the *Buffalo Express*, met up with Townsend at Mathew Brady's National Portrait Gallery at 625 Pennsylvania Avenue. A presence in Washington for nearly two decades, Brady's photo credits included presidents, first ladies, diplomats, generals, artisans, senators, soldiers, street scenes of Washington, Civil War battlefields and literary men. "The Gallery contains a collection of American and European Celebrities, unrivaled on the continent," read Brady's recurring advertisements in the paper. "Portraits of Eminent Men and Women on exhibition for sale."

Twain, Townsend and David Gray, an editor at the *Buffalo Courier*, sat for a photograph that would preserve their brief moment together for perpetuity. In Brady's logbook, held by the Library of Congress, the three men, breaking from custom, sign their own names. Their signatures are the last three on the page.

In the photograph, Twain sits in the middle, leaning back on a leather-cushioned chair, his bow tie askew. His left leg crosses over his right, his hands and fingers coming together in his lap, interlocking. Twain's head is slightly turned to his left side, toward Gray. Twain's brow is mildly furrowed between his amber mop of hair and moustache. He eyes are stern, betraying no inclination of humor, as he looks straightforward. Sitting flat-footed, his eyes looking downward toward the floor, Gray is sitting at the edge of his chair. His hands are gloved, with his right hand resting on Twain's left shoulder. The look on Gray's countenance is of remoteness, of being lost in the moment or unprepared for it. To Twain's right, on a simple wood-frame desk chair turned sideways, is Townsend. His torso is slightly turned left, his head turned enough in that direction to create a profile silhouette. Townsend's right leg crosses over his left, causing his shoe and Twain's shoe to casually brush up against each other. His arms are apart, his left hand gripping the right arm of Twain's chair. His glare is self-assured. Townsend wears a striped tie, his coat buttoned underneath a corsage. Like Twain, Townsend appears to be self-contained, awaiting his own photograph to be taken, unmindful of the two men to his right. According to an entry made on the next page, "17 C.C. sent complimentary"; it appears Brady sent seventeen complimentary prints to Twain.

After the photograph was taken, the trio stuck together and attended a dinner that evening given by New York congressman Samuel Sullivan Cox in Twain's honor at Welcker's Restaurant, the scene of the correspondents' dinner held in January 1868, during which Twain had made a widely reported toast. At the dinner was a collection of elected officials and journalists. Among the group of literary men was Ohio native Donn Piatt, with whom Townsend had recently launched the *Sunday Capital*. Receiving a telegram that his wife, Olivia Langdon Clemens, was ill, Twain had to cut short his dinner plans. Early the next month, Twain wrote to his friend John Henry Riley recapping his recent stopover in Washington: "Was in Washington nearly a month ago. [Adolph] Sutro accused me of sending you abroad." Riley would later die of blood poisoning after his return to the United States from South Africa where he had been in an arrangement with Twain to collaborate on a travel book exploring the diamond business. "So did George Alfred T." Twain added, "The latter says Ramsdell went to San Domingo with the U.S. Commissioners for the NY *Tribune* & left Washington when his wife was within 2 days of her confinement —& G.A.T. says the Row boys will give him the cold shoulder when he gets back."

The extent and degree of Townsend and Twain's relationship is still largely unknown. The single photograph of the men together and their lone correspondence indicates the men remained friends, which is a testament to Twain, who notoriously turned on people. Writing from Hartford on February 26 (the exact date is unknown, but it is most likely 1880 or 1881), Twain offered Townsend praise for his recent book, *Tales of the Chesapeake*. Townsend was actively soliciting reviews, also sending a letter to Frederick Douglass seeking his insights and thoughts on the same book. "My dear Friend," Twain wrote, "Many thanks for the book. I got it yesterday evening and gave it a chance toward bedtime, but it failed to put me to sleep or even make me drowsy. Few books treat me so unkindly. I read it more than half through, picking out the plums, such as 'The Big Idiot,' 'The Circuit

Preacher,' etc. and greatly enjoyed the entertainment. Thank you again. I will respond when my book comes out, George Alfred." Twain signed off, "Your friend, S.L. Clemens." Townsend used this review quote on subsequent editions of the book above praise from other notable literary men and President Rutherford B. Hayes.

Some years later, Townsend interviewed Twain during one of his many excursions to Washington to "talk before one of the committees" on copyright. Townsend wrote:

> *I looked at Mark Twain with a mild interest. Eighteen years ago, I first met him in this city before he was married, when he was writing a few letters to the newspapers for $25 apiece. He had just returned from his trip to Europe and foreign lands, and boarded in a plain house in Washington, and was embarrassed to get possession of the letters which he had published, which his newspaper employers had copyrighted and were indisposed to give him. He got the letters at last and issued his book, and he met about the same time his wife. He is now gray but hale-looking, but he can be quite entertaining when he desires.*

Two decades after George Alfred Townsend and Mark Twain sat together for a photograph by Mathew Brady, the fleeting connections they had during their lives continued. Sometime in the early 1890s, Townsend returned to Brady's recently reopened studio in Washington, fresh on the heels of Twain's visit. When Townsend asked what Twain had to say, Brady reported, "He looked over everything visible, but of course not the unframed copies of my works, and he said: 'Brady, if I was not so tied up in my enterprises I would join you upon this material in which there is a fortune. A glorious gallery to follow that engraved by Sartain and cover the expiring mighty period of American men can be had out of these large, expressive photographs; it would make the noblest subscription book of the age.'"

The Pen Is Mightier Than the Sword

As a reporter in Washington City, Townsend was known to engage in fisticuffs with other reporters. In photos taken of Townsend as a young man in Washington after the Civil War, he is conspicuously wearing gloves. Was he fashioning himself as a pugilist of the press? Later in life, Townsend adopted Richelieu's famous adage, "The Pen Is Mightier Than the Sword," as his own; widely sold cigar tins used this phrase with "GATH" emblazoned on a medieval sword. Townsend had a lightning rod custom-made as a hybrid between a quill pen and sword installed at his summer retreat in the mountains of Maryland. For Townsend, the pen was mighty, but if the situation called for it, his fists could also be mighty.

"Mr. Walker, of the 'Chicago Times,' Looks for 'Gath,' and Finds Him" was the subhead for a small article on the front page of the *Evening Star* in early March 1874. William Sawyer Walker, of the *Chicago Times*, "who for some time past has been engaged in the business of libeling public

George Alfred Townsend, wearing gloves in this photograph, was known to get in fisticuffs on Newspaper Row. *Library of Congress.*

men, private ladies, and his brother correspondents, received a severe castigation this morning at the hands of Mr. George Alfred Townsend," reported the *Star*. "The affair took place at one of the newspaper offices on 14th street, in which Mr. Townsend and Walker accidentally met, and was caused by a statement forwarded to the *Chicago Times* by Walker, to the effect that Townsend lives in a house given to him by the 'Washington ring' to purchase his commendation. Mr. Townsend, on encountering Walker this morning, charged him with writing the falsehood, at the same time saying that when he (Walker) came to Washington, he (Townsend) had befriended him, and that his kindness has been repaid by an infamous libel upon him." Walker tried to explain himself, but Townsend was unmoved and continued his questioning. "Walker, wincing under this onslaught, said he was 'looking for him' (Townsend) yesterday, as he wanted to have a talk with him, and added that he received the information which he sent to the *Times* from his (Townsend's) office. Mr. Townsend thereupon called him a liar, and seizing Walker's umbrella followed it up with a number of vigorous blows. Walker grasped the umbrella and began to retreat." The *New York Times*, reprinting a story from the *Chicago Tribune*, a paper Townsend contributed Washington letters to, reported that Walker scurried under a desk. "It would probably have gone hard with Walker had it not been for Mr. James Holland, of the Associated Press, who happened to be present and who, assuming the role of the peace maker, separated the combatants, thus saving further effusion of blood. Walker was severely punished, and Townsend escaped untouched. Walker probably concludes that 'Gath' is capable of vigorous hitting from the shoulder as well as with the pen."

CHAPTER 14

Washington City's Old Curiosity Shop

I read a good deal, and shall be in nearly every day; and I would be sorry to have
you think me a customer who talks too much and buys too little.
—*"Laura Hawkins" in* The Gilded Age: A Tale of Today

Upon entering Capitol Hill Books at 657 C Street SE, across from Eastern Market, a message warns, "CELL PHONE ADDicts: Read Before Entering → A Bookstore — NOT A PHONE BOOTH. NO CELL PHONE CONVERSATIONS iNSiDE THis BOOKSTORE."

Inside, retired navy admiral Jim Toole greets everyone dryly on cue. Without looking up from penciling a price on his latest acquisition, he directs, "Fiction upstairs, non-fiction down—with many exceptions." From the floor to the ceiling, tens of thousands of books cram the shelves, basement, bathroom, windows, closets and stairs. If one is not careful, towers of books easily avalanche, enveloping people whole. Yells for help are not answered; you should have gotten out of your own way, Toole thinks but does not say.

A fixture on the Hill since 1994, Toole does not suffer fools. "People say I should be nicer to people, but the people are just trying to get books from me on the cheap," Toole says. "I have notes posted throughout the shop. Rule number one: The customer is not always right, I am."

Of the popular independent bookstores in Washington, D.C.— Riverby Books on East Capitol Street SE, Second Story Books just off Dupont Circle, Bridge Street Books on the edge of Georgetown, Idle Time Books on Eighteenth Street NW in Adams Morgan, Politics

Laura Hawkins visits a Washington bookstore in *The Gilded Age: A Tale of Today*. *Author's collection.*

& Prose on upper Connecticut Avenue NW, to name a few—Capitol Hill Books and Toole most resemble the Old Curiosity Shop and its cantankerous proprietor, James Guild, from the late nineteenth and early twentieth centuries of Washington City. Guild did not spare any of his customers, including Twain, an Admiral Toole-like reception.

During Mark Twain's short-lived career as a capital correspondent, he explored the city's "principal bookstores." His first book, *The Jumping Frog*, a collection of Twain's western journalistic work and humorous sketches, was sold in bookstores that lined Pennsylvania Avenue. As young authors still do today, Twain surely visited these stores and asked after his book. Not every shop owner was impressed.

"London may have its Old Curiosity Shop, a building no longer used for the purpose its name indicates but famous as the locality that forms the title, motive, and basis for one of Dickens' masterpieces," wrote a city reporter in 1902. "Washington also has an Old Curiosity Shop worthy of the name, a place that is curious from top to bottom and from end to end, full of curious things, owned by a curious man, conducted on a curious plan." In Arlington National Cemetery's Section 2, near the Chaplains Hill and Monuments, rests the headstone for that "curious man." A plain engraving reads, "JAMES GUILD 3rd Lt. 7 Battn. D.C. Mil. Inf. Died Jan. 19, 1916. Aged 95 Years."

During his lifetime, Guild, who arrived in Washington City in the 1850s from Philadelphia, wore many hats. He was president of the first Stonecutter's Union after working on the first section of the Washington Monument and new wings of the Capitol; army officer in the first company to be raised in the District in 1862; and proprietor, for more than four decades, of a transcendent used bookstore that became the haunt of generals, diplomats, senators, congressmen, journalists, everyday bibliophiles and literary men, including Mark Twain.

After mustering out of the military, Guild "started in the mercantile business" and opened a furniture store at Twelfth and B Streets, near the Washington Canal. A prominent advertisement in the 1867 city directory declares, "New and second-hand furniture, and house keeping articles of every description, sold or exchanged. Repairing, upholstering and varnishing strictly attended to." Later that fall, he relocated his shop to 106 Pennsylvania Avenue NW. According to recurring announcements in the city's daily papers, Guild removed to the "southeast corner of Second Street and Pennsylvania Avenue, where he will be happy to see all his old customers and make as many new ones as possible." Around the same time, in late November 1867, Mark Twain came to Washington City to serve as secretary for Nevada senator William Stewart and to try his hand as a capital correspondent for a number of newspapers.

In the shadow of the U.S. Capitol, Guild rose every morning, seven days a week, to stack a "melee of books, magazines and pictures" from "the dark mysterious interior" of his shop on the curbside. "This is the daily exhibition which never fails to attract the public." On his way to and from the press gallery in the winter of 1867–68, it is within reason to speculate that Mark Twain, then in his early thirties and "green," would have first made contact with Guild, who was as easily greeted by the Speaker of the House as by one of his brothers-in-arms.

Government being the business of Washington, Guild, once he gazed up from whatever tome he was reading at the time and began talking, pulled no punches extolling the benefits of his independence. "You see, they all know I've got no ax to grind, ain't hunting office and wouldn't take a government job if they presented it," he said. "They know they can come here, and I don't take advantage of knowing them. Just like my friend who kept stoves in Lincoln's days. The President would drop in there and sit for hours at a time to keep away from the crowd."

However inconspicuous Guild perceived himself or his shop to be, he was widely known throughout the region and the country as a top-rate auctioneer and for his unique bookshop. In Thomas Fleming's 1902 book, *Around the Capital with Uncle Hank*, the store is immortalized in both picture and prose:

> *Leaving the Capitol grounds, the first thing to catch the eye is a quaint old second-hand book store on the right-hand side of the street, the proprietor of which stands in his cave of volumes like a hibernating bear. Here you will often see statesmen stop on their way to the Capitol to examine some rare book which has accidently caught the eye, and then to bargain with the dealer for its possession. But if the volume in question should be found to possess any merit, rest assured it will not be secured without a payment fully equal to its value, for however unassuming the old book dealer may seem, he is quite adept in price-listing his wares.*

That same year, a *Post* reporter described the store's physical characteristics: "This, the real curiosity shop of Washington, is located in an old-fashioned three-story brick building on lower Pennsylvania Avenue, a structure built many years before the war, with gable roof, attic, and curious little windows that peer out through the roof like so many molehills. Entering this quaint old

"Inside the Old Curiosity Shop." *Around the Capital with Uncle Hank*, 1902. *Collection of John DeFerrari.*

house, one finds it literally packed and jammed with books, magazines, state and government papers, oil paintings, watercolors, steel engravings, objects of art, and pieces of old-fashioned china and silverware." (Guild was often called on to auction off items such as Revolutionary-era munitions as well as

Turkish, Persian and "elegant and varied collections of Oriental wares.") No space went unused. The story continued, "Even the stairs are crowded by piles of literature on either side, affording only a narrow pathway to the top floor up or down, which only one person can pass at a time. Moreover, these books, pictures, and objects of arts are piled, stacked, scattered, strewn, and tumbled about in the most complete and thorough disorder." To administer some semblance of order to the Curiosity Shop's contents "would take two men six or perhaps eight months of steady work, day in and day out." On second thought, "it is more likely that a year would be sufficient."

Guild, now nearing his eightieth year and going blind, was "the sole inmate of this wilderness of literature and art." Despite owning a property in the 900 block of Pennsylvania Avenue NW, Guild slept most nights in a room in the rear of the bookshop where he could cook and eat his meals. In the twilight of life, Guild showed no signs of slowing down, respected as the patriarch of the city's book merchants who, by 1905, were more than twenty strong. It was the Curiosity Shop where "the literati of Washington resorted in search of rare volumes, and the great men of the nation stopped on their way to and from the Capitol."

Mark Twain, the most famous American man of letters, was one of the most well-known visitors to the bookstore. During his decades of visits to the city to lobby for a new copyright law, Twain frequently stopped by the shop, where Guild did not particularly take a liking to him, refusing to treat him like a literary celebrity.

"Was Mark Twain ever here?" a reporter once inquired.

"You mean that Clements [*sic*] man? I don't think much of either him or his books. First time he came here he walked in, 'I'm Mr. Clements [*sic*],' says he. 'Well, an' the devil,' says I. 'You must have heard of my books,' says he. 'I write under the name of Mark Twain.' 'No,' says I, and went on with my reading. He tries to be funny, that man does. I tell you the fun in his books is forced out."

As ambassadors, schoolchildren, writers and politicians continued to patronize the shop, Guild rarely budged from the groove in his worn chair, often paying his customers no mind until they were ready to pay. "I seldom bother to ask their names; in fact, I never bother," Guild admitted, although he was always cooperative with police if they had collared a book thief leaving his store.

By the summer of 1910, Guild was blind and fighting old age in his son's souvenir shop just three stores down from the Curiosity Shop. "I feel better today. I must open the shop," he told a city reporter. "They're his books,"

Alexander Guild said. "He's been with 'em going on forty year[s] now, and it's not for me to open the shop to customers just to sell books. I'd not let one be touched with him lying there sick. No, the shop won't open anymore unless he can open it."

To their consternation, after fielding constant inquiries and well wishes, Alexander, a member of the Association of Oldest Inhabitants, told the senators and congressmen his father's shop was unlikely to reopen. By the end of 1910, the senior Guild decided to close for good and liquidate what remained of his collection. Proceeds from

James Guild, respected proprietor of the Old Curiosity Shop for more than three decades, was not a fan of Twain, who visited his store during his Washington sojourns. *Washington Times,* June 7, 1910. *Library of Congress.*

the once-in-a-lifetime sale injected new capital into Alexander's souvenir and novelty shop at 111 Pennsylvania Avenue NW, where his father spent the last years of his life. With James Guild's death on January 19, 1916, and quiet interment in Arlington National Cemetery, the history of a transformative era in Washington City that was indexed with the names of Garfield, Blaine, and Reed—all Guild confidants—was bookended. Today, the National Museum for the American Indian dominates the city square that once housed Guild's shop.

In epitaphs of the Old Curiosity Shop, it was remarked that Guild was as much a draw for visitors as were his books. At Capitol Hill Books, Toole, nearing his eighties, keeps Guild's spirit of "crotchety" old Washington booksellers alive and well.

"I was in the navy thirty years, twenty-six days and two hours. Retired as a rear admiral. I was an American history major at UCLA," Toole says. "Since I knew I was going into the navy, I thought I ought to know a lot about the country. Then, during night watch, I read up on what we were trying to do internationally and how it was influenced by history. I eventually received a master's in International Relations from American University. I have been reading nonfiction for sixty years. They don't teach that [expletive] any more. Instead they teach American Studies. Kids

Jim Toole at Capitol Hill Books, June 2013. *Photo by author.*

nowadays know nothing about their history; it is blended with sociology and American Studies."

Breaking his stern demeanor, Toole says with a wry grin, "I tell these kids who come in my shop saying, 'Like this' and 'Like that,' 'Life is not a simile.' I give away copies of the thesaurus for free."

CHAPTER 15
The Prince of Lobbyists

To promote the Progress of Science and useful Arts, by securing for limited Times to Authors and Inventors the exclusive Right to their respective Writings and Discoveries.
—United States Constitution, Article 1, Section 8

For decades following his emergence and establishment as one of the most popular American writers of his generation, Mark Twain was a frequent presence, by himself and with other literary men, in and around the halls of Congress; he frequently met with members and their staffs to argue on behalf of enhanced author rights and protections. He is most commonly portrayed today in popular culture and exists in our collective consciousness as the "man in the white suit." In December 1906 in Washington, at the Library of Congress, Twain first introduced that definitive look that has been seared and perpetuated into our memories. The preparation for his role as a lead player on the national stage of copyright law had been decades in the making, with the dress rehearsals occurring in Washington, D.C.

The story of the "grand literary storehouse" at the Library of Congress as the ultimate keeper of copyrights began in June 1870 when President Grant signed a bill that Ainsworth Spofford, Librarian of Congress from 1865 to 1897, had advocated for. The bill made the Library of Congress the central agency for copyright registration and the central repository for copyrighted material in the country. In 1790, Congress passed the first copyright law, creating the Library of Congress, housed in the United States Capitol until 1897. The 1870 law required "all authors, poets, artists, composers, and mapmakers to deposit [at

Ainsworth Rand Spofford (1825–1908), sixth Librarian of Congress, 1864–97. *Library of Congress.*

the Library of Congress] two copies of every book, pamphlet, map, print, and piece of music registered in the United States."

The driving force behind the 1870 bill was Ainsworth Rand Spofford. According to John Y. Cole, Spofford was a bookseller, abolitionist pamphleteer and literary essayist before coming to Washington in 1861 as a correspondent for the *Cincinnati Commercial.* After becoming the Assistant Librarian of Congress shortly after arriving in Washington, Spofford was promoted to the Librarian of Congress before the conclusion of the Civil War. In the *Union Catalog of Clemens Letters*, which includes thousands of items of Mark Twain's correspondence, there are nearly two dozen letters between Twain and Spofford. The first known letter Twain sent Spofford was from Buffalo, New York, in October 1870 asking to "preserve" his well-known "Fortification of Paris" woodcut as a "work of art among the geographical treasures of the Congressional Library." As the editors of the Mark Twain Papers suggest, "The informality of Clemens's request, his first known letter to Spofford, suggests that the two men were already acquainted, probably since late 1867 and early 1868, when Clemens lived in Washington." In 1875, Twain sent Spofford a news clipping from the *New York Times* that read, "The performance of a play was not a publication within the meaning of the Copyright Law." Twain asked, "Will you be so kind as to tell me whether the above is correct or erroneous?" The query from Twain was enclosed in a letter marked private that explained "[t]hree different parties have tried to pirate the 'Gilded Age' & I wish to know if I have at last left a loophole to open."

Between 1865 and 1897, the years of Spofford's tenure, "copyright deposit added to the library's collection approximately 350,000 books and pamphlets, 47,000 maps and charts, 250,000 musical compositions, 12,000 engravings, lithographs, and chromolithographs, 33,000 photographs, 3,000 etchings,

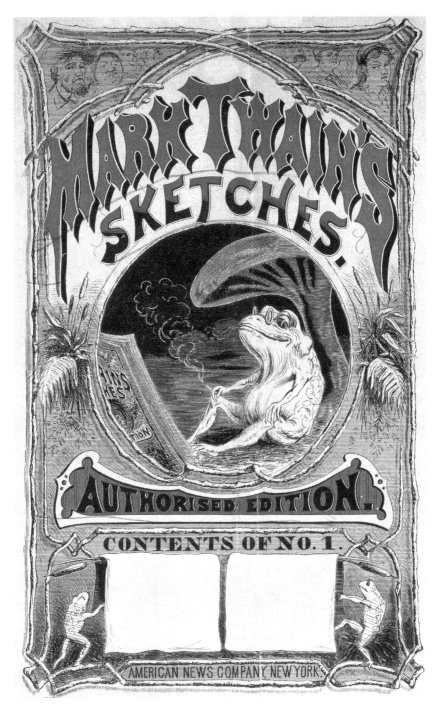

Book cover for which Mark Twain sought a copyright in 1874. *Library of Congress*.

Copyright deposits in the basement in need of shelving. *Library of Congress.*

and 6,000 dramatic compositions." As Cole writes, "The centralization of copyright activities at the Library of Congress not only developed impressive collections but also gave the library an exclusive government function and the national prestige which naturally accompanied it. For the first time, the Library became a part of the publishing and, to a lesser extent, the literary world." As a result, the library "came at last to be generally recognized as a national institution."

During his tenure as Librarian of Congress, Spofford was the "the sole copyright officer of the U.S. Government" and regularly corresponded with "statesmen, scholars, and literary figures all over the United States, as well as with publishers and editors." In retirement, he presented lectures before the Columbia Historical Society, today the Historical Society of Washington. Papers Spofford presented to the society such as "The Life and Labors of Peter Force, Mayor of Washington" and "Washington in Literature" are demonstrative of the scholarship and commitment to letters that defined him and his era. It was an age Mark Twain helped shape.

"Mark Twain goes down every winter to work for the passage of an international copyright law in conjunction with Edward Eggleston, [William Henry] Gilder, and other authors," recorded an 1889 article in the *New*

York Herald. "Senator Reagan, of Texas, a friend of Mark's but an opponent of his pet measure, greeted him cordially last winter with 'How are you, Mark?' How are you? Right glad to see you! Glad to see you! Hope to see you every session as long as you live!'" When turned away by unsympathetic legislators, Twain turned to one of his "favorite amusements," which was to become "an amateur guide and [explain] to his friends the various objects of interest in the Capitol." Twain was reportedly "particularly facetious over the pictures in the rotunda and the stone people in 'Statuary' Hall. Arriving opposite to the marble statue of Fulton, seated and intently examining the model of a steamboat in his hands, he indulges in a wide sweeping gesture and exclaims: 'This, ladies and gentlemen, is Pennsylvania's favorite son, Robert Fulton. Observe his easy and unconventional attitude. Notice his serene and contented expression caught by the artist at the moment when he made up his mind to steal John Fitch's steamboat.'"

Returning to Congress twenty years after his stint as a capital correspondent, now a successful and prolific author, Twain was dressed better, but his mannerisms and diction remain unchanged. "The humorist dresses a good deal more carefully than formerly. This is made necessary by his increasing amplitude, his vast shock of gray hair, by his boisterous and ungovernable mustache and by his turbulent eyebrows that cover his

Mark Twain was at the front of American authors lobbying for a strengthened copyright. *Punch Magazine,* 1886. *Library of Congress.*

gray eyes like a dissolute thatch. And when he talks, he talks slowly and extracts each of his vowels with a corkscrew twist that would make even the announcement of a funeral sound like a joke."

In January 1905, Mark Twain took his copyright concerns public in the *North American Review* with "An Open Letter to the Register of Copyrights." Twain wrote to the Register of Copyrights, "I have received your excellent summary of the innumerable statutes and substitutes and amendments which a Century of Congresses have devised in trying to mete out even-handed justice to the public and the author in the vexed matter of copyright." Responding to an "invitation to the craftsmen of my guild to furnish suggestions for further legislation upon the subject," Twain offered an "unconventional" answer in the form of "Question and Answer." He asked and answered his own questions.

Question: "How many new American books are copyrighted annually in the United States?" Answer: "Five or six thousand." After crunching the numbers of how many books had been published since 1800, Twain advanced that of those quarter million books, an average of five per year—"ten, to be safe and certain"—had "survived or will survive the 42-year limit." In other words, most books would have fallen out of print forty-two years after their first publication, but at least ten books would still be in print, potentially generating royalties for their authors for more than forty-two years. The authors of these long-running books, authors like Twain, were denied the proceeds by the current forty-two-year expiration of the copyright law.

When Twain asked himself what the forty-two-year limit on copyright accomplished, he responded, "Nothing useful, nothing worthy, nothing modest, nothing dignified, so far as I know. An Italian statesman has called it 'the Countess Massiglia of legal burlesque.' Each year, ten venerable copyrights fall in, and the bread of ten persons is taken from them by the Government." Although Twain recognized this as "small business," it was still, in his mind, "a distinct reversal of the law of the survival of the fittest. It is the assassination of the fittest." To protect against the manslaughter and extortion of his work into indiscriminate "cheap editions," Twain sought the help of allies in Congress, an institution he berated throughout his life.

One of Twain's closest Congressional allies was Champ Clark, representative from Missouri. As Clark recalled in his memoirs, "[H]e wrote to me stating that he wanted a bill passed giving to authors a perpetual copyright. I answered, explaining that the Congress would never enact any such law—also stating that he employ a good lawyer to work out a

House Speaker Champ Clark, President William Howard Taft, House Speaker Joseph Cannon and ex-governor of Massachusetts Samuel W. McCall. *Library of Congress.*

bill containing my suggestions." Twain followed Clark's counsel, and a law was drawn up "marking more liberal arrangements to copyright, thereby largely enhancing their value." Twain wrote back that he was coming to Washington to lobby for the bill. According to Clark, Twain was the "prince of lobbyists." Twain was, in fact, no stranger to using his influence in commenting "editorially on [legislative] proceedings." According to esteemed Twain scholar Henry Nash Smith, while covering Nevada's Constitutional Convention as a reporter for the Virginia City *Territorial Enterprise* in the summer of 1863, Twain first gained "confidence in his powers as a lobbyist."

By December 1906, the stage was set for Mark Twain's most memorable performance. Finding himself in the Capitol and engaged in light conversation with Clark, Twain wanted to harden the talk and discuss his bill with those who held votes on the Committee of Patents. Clark had a solitary room at his disposal while Speaker Joseph Cannon had a handful of accommodations. Clark "borrowed one of [Cannon's] stenographer's rooms on the ground floor and sent a page up into the House to notify certain members that Mark Twain was below and desired to converse with them." The legislators soon began to seek out the source of the commotion. "[I]n fact, first and last they nearly all came, and for two days Twain held his court—talking all the time—and such talk!" According to Clark, "He talked about steamboating on the Mississippi, about his experiences in Nevada, California, and the Sandwich Islands, about lecturing, writing books, about his travels in far lands, about getting rich and going broke, about the prominent people he had met—in short, about almost everything and everybody—but always wound up by arguing in favor of his bill." According to Paine, "In an atmosphere blue with tobacco smoke, Mark Twain talked the gospel of copyright to his heart's content" until "the daylight faded and the rest of the Capitol grew still."

In the hours leading up to the copyright hearing at the Library of Congress, Twain visited Speaker Cannon's office. "There was no altruistic humbug about him," Cannon recalled years later. "He wanted to go on the floor of the House to lobby, but those confounded 'Cannon Rules' prohibited him, and they likewise so bound the Speaker that he could not recognize another Member to ask unanimous consent to admit Mark Twain or any other man to the floor." Years before, in 1888, Twain, after having "swapped lies" with the new generation of capital correspondents in the press gallery, had been admitted to the House floor by Ohio representative Samuel Cox, a longtime advocate. "[Twain] kept the crowd of members around him laughing until the gavel of the speaker came to the rescue of order," reported the *Hartford Courant*. "He says that the levee that he had reminds him very much of those he used to see on the Mississippi on those days when he was piloting."

Like previous Speakers, Twain had encountered, Cannon was no pushover, but this time Twain thought he might be on the receiving end of a special favor. "Mark studied those rules and discovered that the only exception made was to those who had received the thanks of Congress. So he wrote to me and, acting as his own messenger, came to my room one cold morning and laid the letter on my desk."

Dec. 7, 1906

Dear Uncle Joseph,

Please get me the thanks of the Congress—not next week but right away. It is very necessary. Do accomplish this for your affectionate old friend right away; by persuasion if you can, by violence if you must, for it is imperatively necessary that I get on the floor for two or three hours and talk to the members, man by man, on behalf of the support, encouragement and protection of one of the nation's most valuable assets and industries— its literature. I have arguments with me, also a barrel, with liquid in it. Give me a chance. Give me the thanks of Congress. Don't wait for others; there isn't time. I have stayed away and let Congress alone for seventy-one years, and I am entitled to thanks. Congress knows it perfectly well, and I have long felt hurt that this quite proper and earned expression of gratitude has been merely felt by the House and never publicly uttered. Send me an order on the Sergeant-at-Arms quick, When shall I come? With love and a benediction,

Mark Twain

But "'Uncle Joe' could not give him the privilege of the floor; the rules had become more stringent. He declared that they would hang him if he did such a thing." Nonetheless, Twain would create his moment to shine.

At half past three in the afternoon, Mark Twain walked the halls of the Library of Congress and entered the hearing of the joint Congressional committee in charge of the newly proposed copyright bill. Twain was led to his seat among the "literary group" by Hebert Putnam, the chief librarian. Before taking his seat, Twain removed his overcoat to reveal a white flannel suit, which caused "a perceptible stir." After remarks by Dr. Edward Everett Hale, chaplain of the Senate, Twain rose as the last witness of the day. "He did not stand by his chair as the others had done, but he walked over to the Speaker's table and, turning, faced his audience," Paine recalls. "The weary committee, which had been tortured all day with dull, statistical arguments made by the mechanical-deice fiends and dreary platitudes unloaded by men whose chief ambition was to shine as copyright champions, suddenly realized that they were being rewarded for the long waiting." Members of the committee "began to brighten and freshen, and uplift a smile like flowers that have been wilted by a drought when comes the refreshing shower that means renewed life and vigor."

As William Dean Howells, Twain's lifelong friend, recalled, Twain cut quite a figure. "[T]he white serge was an inspiration which few men would have had the courage to act upon," Howells declared. "The first time I saw him wear it was at the authors' hearing before the Congressional Committee in Washington. Nothing could have been more dramatic than the gestures with which he flung off his long loose overcoat and stood forth in white from his feet to the crown of his silvery head. It was a magnificent coup, and he dearly loved a coup; but the magnificent speech which he made, tearing to shreds the venerable farrago of non-sense about non-property in ideas which had formed the basis of all copyright legislation, made you forget even his spectacularity."

Peacock Alley at today's Willard Hotel. *Photo by author.*

Without speaking from notes, Twain began, "I am particularly interested in the portion of the measure which concerns my trade. I like that extension from the present limit of the life copyright from forty-two years to the life of the author and fifty years thereafter." He continued, "I think that ought to satisfy any reasonable author because it will take care of his children—let the grandchildren take care of themselves." Twain was not just advocating for literary craftsmen, but all artisans. "It is not objectionable to me that all the trades and industries of the United States are in the bill and protected by it. I should like to have the oyster culture added, and anything else that might need protection. I have no ill feeling." When Twain concluded his remarks, "applause came like an explosion."

Following Twain's remarks, "a universal rush of men and women to get near enough for a word and to shake his hand" came forward. Despite the attention, Twain was anxious to make an exit. Along with his biographer, Albert Bigelow Paine, Twain drove down Pennsylvania Avenue to the Willard, talking and smoking and preparing for dinner. "He was elated and said the occasion required full-dress," Paine remembered. "We started down at last, fronted and frocked like penguins. I did not realize then the fullness of his for theatrical effect. I supposed he would go down with as little ostentation as possible, so I took him by the elevator which enters the dining room without passing through the long corridor known as 'Peacock Alley' because of its being a favorite place for handsomely dressed fashionable of the national capital." When Paine and Twain reached the entrance of the dining room, Twain said, "Isn't there another chance to this place?" Paine replied that there was but that they would have to go down a long corridor. "Oh, well," Twain said, "I don't mind that. Let's go back and try it over." The two men took the elevator back up, walked to the other end of the hotel and came down to the F Street entrance. "There is a fine, stately flight of steps—a really royal stair—leading from this entrance down into 'Peacock Alley.' To slowly descend that flight is an impressive thing to do," Paine wrote. "It is like descending the steps of a throne-room or to some royal landing-place where Cleopatra's barge might lie." Twain stepped in style, drawing the attention of "feminine admirers" and making "passage along the corridor" a "perpetual gantlet." The dinner was a "continuous reception."

Before returning to New York, Twain wanted to make a special site visit in Washington. Paine recalled, "In New York, I had once brought him a print of the superb 'Adams Memorial' by Saint-Gaudens—the bronze woman who sits in the still court in the Rock Creek Cemetery in Washington." During one of their last mornings in Washington, Twain

Late in life, Twain took a carriage to visit the Adams Memorial, sculpted by Augustus Saint-Gaudens, in Rock Creek Cemetery. *Library of Congress.*

made a request: "Engage a carriage and we will drive out and see the Saint-Gaudens bronze." It was a "bleak, dull December day, and as we walked down through the avenues of the dead, there was a presence of unrealized sorrow that seemed exactly suited to such a visit. We entered the little inclosure [*sic*] of cedars where sits the dark figure which is art's supreme express of great human mystery of life and death. Instinctively, we removed our hats, and neither spoke until we had come away." Twain broke the silence, asking solemnly, "What does he call it?" Paine did not know but "had heard applied to it that great line of Shakespeare's—'the rest is silence.'" Twain rebutted, "But that figure is not silent." Twain later remarked, "It is in deep meditation on sorrowful things." According to Paine, "When we returned to New York, he had the little print framed and kept it always on his mantelpiece." Today, the statue is commonly known as "Grief," and legend has it that Twain is the source of the sobriquet. While in Washington as a capital correspondent, Twain wrote John Russell Young, editor of the *New York Tribune*, "I am sorry to trouble you so much, but behold the world is full of sorrows, & grief is the heritage of man."

The copyright extension Twain sought was not ultimately adopted by Congress until 1909. When the law passed, Champ Clark wrote to Twain seeking his opinion. Writing from Redding, Connecticut, Twain opened his note, "Is the new copyright law acceptable to me? Emphatically, yes! Clark, it is the only sane, and clearly defined, and just and righteous copyright law that has ever existed in the United States. Whosoever will compare it with its predecessors will have no trouble in arriving at that decision." Two years before, Twain had written:

> *When I was down there was the most stupefying jumble of conflicting and apparently irreconcilable interests that was ever seen; and we all said, "The case is hopeless, absolutely hopeless—out of this chaos nothing can be built." But we were in error; out of that chaotic mass this excellent bill has been instructed; the warring interests have been reconciled, and the result is as comely and substantial a legislative edifice as lifts its domes and towers and protective lightning rods out of the statute book, I think. When I think of that other bill, which even the Deity couldn't understand, and of this one which even I can understand, I take off my hat to the man or men who devised this one.*

Although rather overlooked in the telling of Twain's whirlwind life by biographers, Washington, D.C., was a pivotal place for the man of letters. He came to the capital in the winter of 1867–68 as a bohemian journalist and became a legitimate author who would grow into arguably the most prominent and, inarguably, the most popular American novelist. His experiences in Washington, D.C., were seminal in his development and maturation as a writer and storyteller over more than a half century and in

Mark Twain premiered his trademark white suit at a copyright hearing at the Library of Congress in December 1906. *Library of Congress.*

his final coup-de-grace in securing his, as well as other artists' and artisans', legal legacy. In the end, even now from the grave, Mark Twain manages to have the final word.

Selected Bibliography

BOOKS AND OTHER WRITINGS

Benson, Ivan. *Mark Twain's Western Years*. New York: Russell & Russell, 1966.

Bliss, Donald T. *Mark Twain's Tale of Today: Halley's Comet Returns—The Celebrated Author Critiques American Politics*. N.p.: CreateSpace, 2012.

Branch, Edgar Marquess. *The Literary Apprenticeship of Mark Twain*. Urbana: University of Illinois Press, 1950.

Briggs, Emily Edson. *The Olivia Letters; Being Some History of Washington City for Forty Years as Told by the Letters of a Newspaper Correspondent*. New York: The Neale Publishing Company, 1906.

Brown, Letitia Woods. *Free Negroes in the District of Columbia, 1790–1846*. New York: Oxford University Press, 1972.

Budd, Louis J. *Critical Essays on Mark Twain, 1867–1910*. Boston: G.K. Hall, 1982.

Caron, James E. *Mark Twain, Unsanctified Newspaper Reporter*. Columbia: University of Missouri Press, 2008.

Clark, Champ. *My Quarter Century in American Politics*. Volume 2. New York: Harper & Brothers, 1920.

Cole, John Y. *Copyright in the Library of Congress: 125ᵗʰ Anniversary*. Washington, D.C.: Library of Congress, 1995.

Dahlgren, Madeleine Vinton. *Etiquette of Social Life in Washington*. Philadelphia: J.B. Lippincott, 1881.

Dary, David. *Red Blood and Black Ink: Journalism in the Old West*. St. Lawrence: University Press of Kansas, 1999.

de Tocqueville, Alexis. *Democracy in America: The Republic of the United States and Its Political Institutions Reviewed and Examined*. New York: A.S. Barnes & Co., 1855.

Dickens, Charles. *American Notes for General Circulation*. London: Chapman and Hall, 1842.

Emery, Fred A. "Washington Newspaper Correspondents." *Records of the Columbia Historical Society Vol. 35/36*, 1935.

———. "Washington Newspapers." *Records of the Columbia Historical Society Vol. 37/38*, 1937.

Essary, Frederick J. *Covering Washington: Government Reflected to the Public in the Press, 1822–1926*. Boston: Houghton Mifflin Company, 1927.

Fanning, Philip. *Mark Twain and Orion Clemens: Brothers, Partners, Strangers*. Tuscaloosa: University of Alabama Press, 2003.

Fatout, Paul. *Mark Twain on the Lecture Circuit*. Bloomington: Indiana University Press, 1960.

Fishkin, Shelley Fisher. *The Mark Twain Anthology: Great Writers on His Life and Work*. New York: Library of America, 2010.

———. *Was Huck Black? Mark Twain and African-American Voices*. New York: Oxford University Press, 1993.

Frazier, Harriet C. *Runaway and Freed Missouri Slaves and Those Who Helped Them, 1763–1865.* Jefferson, NC: McFarland Company, 2004.

Fulton, Joe B. *The Reconstruction of Mark Twain: How A Confederate Bushwhacker Became the Lincoln of Our Literature.* Baton Rouge: Louisiana State University, 2011.

Gopnick, Adam. "The Man in the White Suit: Why the Mark Twain Industry Keeps Growing." *The New Yorker*, November 29, 2010.

Green, Constance M. *Secret City: History of Race Relations in the Nation's Capital.* Princeton, NJ: Princeton University Press, 1967.

Hindes, Ruthanna. *George Alfred Townsend: One of Delaware's Outstanding Writers.* N.p.: Hambleton Printing & Publishing Company, 1946.

Hines, Christian A. *Early Recollections of Washington City.* Washington, D.C.: Chronicle Book and Job Print, 1866.

Johnston, James H. *From Slave Ship to Harvard: Yarrow Mamout and the History of an African American Family.* New York: Fordham University Press, 2012.

Kaplan, Justin. *Mr. Clemens and Mark Twain: A Biography.* New York: Simon and Schuster, 1967.

Lathrop, George P. "A Nation in a Nutshell." *Harper's Magazine*, March 1881.

Lynch, Anne C. "Sketch of Washington City." *Harper's Magazine*, December 1852.

Mac Donnell, Kevin. "How Samuel Clemens Found 'Mark Twain' in Carson City." *Mark Twain Journal* 50, no. 1–2 (Spring/Fall 2012).

Paine, Albert Bigelow. *Mark Twain: A Biography.* 3 vols. New York: Harper & Brothers, 1912.

Petitt, Arthur G. *Mark Twain and the South.* Lexington: University of Kentucky Press, 1974.

Poore, Benjamin Perley. *Congressional Director for the First Session of the Forty-first Congress of the United States of America.* Washington, D.C.: Government Printing Office, 1869.

———. *Perley's Reminiscences of Sixty Years in the National Metropolis.* Philadelphia: Hubbard Brothers, 1886.

———. "Washington News." *Harper's New Monthly Magazine,* January 1874.

Powers, Ron. *Dangerous Water: A Biography of the Boy Who Became Mark Twain.* New York: Basic Books, 1999.

———. *Mark Twain: A Life.* New York: Simon and Schuster, 2005.

Reigstad, Thomas J. *Scribblin' For A Livin': Mark Twain's Pivotal Period in Buffalo.* Amherst, New York: Prometheus Books, 2013.

Ritchie, Donald A. *Press Gallery: Congress and the Washington Correspondents.* Cambridge, MA: Harvard University Press, 1991.

Scharnhorst, Gary, ed. *Mark Twain: The Complete Interviews.* Tuscaloosa: University of Alabama Press, 2006.

Shields, Jerry. *Gath's Literary Work and Folk: And Other Selected Writings of George Alfred Townsend.* Wilmington, DE: Delaware Heritage Press, 1996.

Smith, Henry Nash. *Mark Twain of the Enterprise.* Berkeley: University of California Press, 1957.

Spofford, Ainsworth Rand. "Washington in Literature." *Records of the Columbia Historical Society Volume 6,* 1903.

Stewart, David O. *Impeached: The Trial of President Andrew Johnson and the Fight for Lincoln's Legacy.* New York: Simon & Schuster, 2009.

Stewart, William M. *Reminiscences of Senator William M. Stewart of Nevada.* New York: Neale Publishing Company, 1908.

Summers, Mark Walhgren. *The Press Gang: Newspapers and Politics, 1865–1878*. Chapel Hill: University of North Carolina Press, 1994.

Townsend, George Alfred. "New Washington." *Harper's Magazine*, February 1875.

———. "Still Taking Pictures: Brady, the Grand Old Man of American Photography." *New York World*, April 12, 1891.

———. *Washington, Outside and Inside: A Picture and a Narrative of the Origin, Growth, Excellences, Abuses, Beauties, and Personages of Our Governing City*. Hartford, CT: James Betts and Co., 1873.

Twain, Mark. *Autobiography of Mark Twain: The Complete and Authoritative Edition*. Berkeley: University of California Press, 2010.

———. "Chapters From My Autobiography I–XXVII." *North American Review*, September 1906–December 1907.

———. "Concerning Copyright: An Open Letter to the Register of Copyrights." *North American Review*, January 1905.

———. *Early Tales & Sketches Volume 1: 1851–1864*. Berkeley: University of California Press, 1979.

———. "Facts Concerning My Resignation." *New York Tribune*, December 27, 1867.

———. "The Facts Concerning the Recent Important Resignation." *New York Tribune*, February 13, 1868.

———. "General Washington's Negro Body-Servant." *Galaxy Magazine*, February 1868.

———. *Letters, 1853–1866, Volume 1*. Berkeley: University of California Press, 1989.

———. *Letters, 1867–1868, Volume 2*. Berkeley: University of California Press, 1990.

———. *Letters, 1870–1871, Volume 4.* Berkeley: University of California Press, 1995.

———. "Mental Telegraphy: A Manuscript with a History." *Harper's Magazine*, December 1891.

———. "My Late Senatorial Secretaryship." *Galaxy Magazine*, May 1868.

———. *Notebooks & Journals, Volume 1: 1855–1873.* Berkeley: University of California Press, 1975.

———. "The Private History of a Campaign that Failed." *Century Magazine*, December 1885.

———. "Riley: Newspaper Correspondent." *Galaxy Magazine*, November 1870.

Warden, David B. *Description of the District of Columbia: A Chorographical and Statistical Description of the District of Columbia, the Seat of the General Government of the United States.* Paris: 1816.

Wiencek, Henry. *An Imperfect God: George Washington, His Slaves and the Creation of America.* New York: Farrar, Straus and Giroux, 2003.

Williams, Wellington. *Appleton's Northern and Eastern Traveler's Guide.* New York: D. Appleton Company, 1852.

Wilson, Robert. *Mathew Brady: Portraits of a Nation.* New York: Bloomsbury, 2013.

Young, James Sterling. *The Washington Community, 1800–1828.* New York: Columbia University Press, 1966.

Collections

Gathland State Park, Maryland Department of Natural Resources.

Historical Society of Washington.

Library of Congress, Manuscript Division.

Selected Bibliography

————. Mearns, David C. "Mark Twain in Washington."

————. John Russell Young Papers.

Mark Twain Project Online, University of California–Berkeley.

Peabody Room, DC Public Library (Georgetown Branch).

Washingtoniana Division, DC Public Library (Martin Luther King Jr. Memorial Library).

Newspapers and Periodicals

Chicago Republican
Daily Alta California
Daily Morning Chronicle
Evening Star
Galaxy Magazine
Georgetown Courier
Harper's Monthly Magazine
Hartford Courant
Mark Twain Journal
National Intelligencer
National Republican
New York Herald
New York Times
New York Tribune
New York World
North American Review
Philadelphia Press
Records of the Columbia Historical Society
San Francisco Evening Bulletin
Virginia City Territorial Enterprise
Washington Critic
Washington History
Washington Post
Washington Times

Index

About the Author

John Muller is an associate librarian at the Washingtoniana Division of the Martin Luther King Jr. Memorial Library and a Washington-based journalist, historian, playwright and policy analyst. His first book, *Frederick Douglass in Washington, D.C.: The Lion of Anacostia*, won a public vote to be selected as the DC Public Library's 2013 DC Reads. A former reporter for the *Washington Times*, Muller is a current contributor  to Capital Community News, Greater Greater Washington and other Washington, D.C.–area media. His writing and reporting has appeared in *Washington History*, the *Washington Post*, the *Georgetowner*, *East of the River*, the *Washington Informer*, DCist, *Suspense Magazine*, Next American City and a forthcoming publication of the German Historical Institute. Muller has covered municipal and neighborhood politics and current affairs in the metropolitan area for the last half-decade. In 2004, Muller co-founded a theater company, DreamCity Theatre Group, that was a finalist for three 2007 Mayor's Arts Awards, including Outstanding Contribution to Arts Education. He is a member of the Historical Society of Washington and serves on the planning committee for the annual D.C. Historical Studies Conference. Muller is a 2007 graduate of George Washington University, with a BA in public policy, and a 1995 graduate of Greenwood Elementary School in Brookeville, Maryland.